Praise for Wendy Lawless and H

CHANEL BONFIRE

"*Chanel Bonfire* makes an undesirable truth more vivid: some mothers just plain suck.... Wendy Lawless survived her mother's flagrant horror show to bear witness and record her astonishing child

"Riveting.. ter, maybe

"Lawless le never desce

"[An] enter bringing."

"Provocativ moving."

"Lawless le memoir."

"Her wit, resilience, and compassion make her story illuminating and inspiring."

—*Reader's Digest*

"A wrought and engaging memoir."

—*Publishers Weekly*

"Heartbreaking. . . . I will never look at a blue nightgown the same way again!"

—Tim Gunn, *New York Times* bestselling author of *Tim Gunn's Fashion Bible*

CHANEL BONFIRE

a memoir

WENDY LAWLESS

GALLERY BOOKS

New York London Toronto Sydney New Delhi

A NOTE TO READERS

Names and identifying details of some of the people portrayed
in this book have been changed.

G

Gallery Books
A Division of Simon & Schuster, Inc.
1230 Avenue of the Americas
New York, NY 10020

First Gallery Books trade paperback edition November 2013

GALLERY BOOKS and colophon are registered trademarks
of Simon & Schuster, Inc.

For information about special discounts for bulk purchases, please contact Simon &
Schuster Special Sales at 1-866-506-1949 or business@simonandschuster.com.

The Simon & Schuster Speakers Bureau can bring authors to your live event. For
more information or to book an event contact the Simon & Schuster Speakers
Bureau at 1-866-248-3049 or visit our website at www.simonspeakers.com.

Designed by Jaime Putorti

Library of Congress Cataloging-in-Publication Data

Lawless, Wendy.
    Chanel bonfire / Wendy Lawless. -- 1st Gallery Books trade paperback ed.
        p. cm.
    Summary: "Wendy Lawless's stunning memoir of resilience in the face of an unstable
alcoholic and suicidal mother"-- Provided by publisher.
    Includes bibliographical references and index.
    1. Lawless, Wendy. 2. Motion picture actors and actresses—United States—
Biography. 3. Actresses—United States—Biography. I. Title.
    PN2287.L28555A3 2013
    791.4302'8092--dc23
    [B]
                            2012011324

ISBN 978-1-4516-7536-8 (hardback)
ISBN 978-1-4767-4548-0 (pbk)
ISBN 978-1-4516-7538-2 (ebook)

Manufactured in the United States of America

10 9 8 7 6 5 4 3 2

To my sister, Robin

CHANEL BONFIRE

NEW YORK, 1969

chapter one

THE BIG SLEEP

Perhaps because her second marriage had only lasted twenty months, or perhaps because she was having a bad hair day, in January of 1969 my mother swallowed a whole bottle of pills and called my stepfather at his hotel to say good-bye.

Although they were still legally married, he had installed himself at the Carlyle while she sued him for divorce. After he received her farewell call, he quickly finished his Gibson, telephoned the fire department, grabbed his Burberry raincoat, and jumped into a taxi. It was a time in New York when you could say to a cabdriver, "Take me to the St. Regis," or, "Take me to the Oak Bar," and he would just take you there—no further explanation was needed. "Take me to the Dakota," he said to the driver.

While my mother arranged herself on her monogrammed, baby-blue satin sheets and prepared to enter the Valley of the Dolls, and my stepfather chain-smoked and shouted at the cabdriver to go faster, goddammit, I slept in the top bunk of the bed I shared with my younger sister, Robin, dreaming of hot dogs.

We had been living in the Dakota, the late nineteenth-century, neo-Gothic apartment house at the corner of Seventy-second Street and Central Park West, for about a year and a half. And while I would later think of the place—the setting for the film *Rosemary's Baby* and the future and final home of John Lennon—as a glamorous backdrop for my mother's tumultuous second marriage and divorce, at the time it was just our rather large and wonderfully spooky apartment, in which I was about to find myself awakened by my mother's rescuers.

I was driven from my hot dog dreamworld by a plinking sound, high and silvery—the sound of something falling, like rain but heavier and coming from inside the house. I got out of bed, carefully climbed down the bunk-bed ladder past my sleeping sister, and walked out into the long hallway of our cavernous apartment. I peeked around the corner to find four firemen in big, dark coats and hats beating down Mother's bedroom door with axes. One of them stood on a ladder breaking the glass in the transom window above the door. The shards of glass rained down on the men below and bounced off their helmets, making a tinkly noise as they hit the polished parquet floor.

I wondered why they didn't use a key or just knock on the door like I did. They were making a big mess, which always made Mother angry. And it was very loud and Mother hated loud noises. ("It's because I'm a Libra," she'd explain.)

Boy, were those firemen going to get it when she opened the door, I thought. They took no notice of me. I turned and looked the other way toward the foyer and saw my stepfather in his raincoat hustling down the hall toward me. I was surprised to see him; I hadn't seen him in a while. Even when he was still living at the apartment, he never seemed to be around.

"Hi, Pop," I said. "Are you coming back?"

"Yes, dearie," he said, uttering another in what was becoming a long series of big fat lies that made up my primary interaction with grown-ups. He didn't look at me as he passed, but he smelled like cologne and French cigarettes. The firemen parted to make way for him and he pounded on the door with his fist.

"Georgann! Open this goddamn door!" he bellowed.

There was silence as everyone held his breath, listening for some sign of life on the other side of the now-battered door. Nothing. My stepfather took a step back, and the men continued to hack through it.

From the far side of all this noise, flying glass, and splintered wood, appeared our nanny, Catherine, a Caribbean giantess in a bathrobe and slippers. Her cold-creamed and bespectacled face bore the look of disapproval and incomprehension with which she regarded almost everything that went on at our house—crazy white people acting crazy. She put her hands on her massive hips and said, "What the blazes is goin' on here?!" The men didn't stop.

Catherine surveyed the chaos until her eyes found me standing there in the hall in my nightgown. Here was something she could do—get the little one back to bed. She raised her eyebrows and began to amble slowly down the hall in my direction.

Catherine, who stayed with us longer than Dinah or Fanny or any of the other nannies, was always trying to put our house in order. I loved her and hated her for that. I loved her because she fed us, bathed us, and rubbed Vicks VapoRub on our chests when we were sick. I hated her because I wanted my mother to do those things for us.

"C'mon now, Wendy," she barked. Her voice was incredibly loud so it always seemed like she was shouting at you. "Time to go."

I looked up at Catherine, towering above me. She was like a mountain with a crown of curlers. Her huge body completely blocked my view of the action. Two more men with dark blue jackets over white uniforms raced by us from the front door, pushing a stretcher on wheels. I tried to watch but Catherine firmly grasped my shoulders and steered me back to my bedroom.

Inside, she shooed me up the bunk-bed ladder, patting me lightly on the bottom. "You go to sleep now, lambie pie," she said, pulling the covers up to my chin.

I could hear her heavy breathing as she leaned in under my bed to fix my sister's kicked-off covers. Robbie could have slept through a train wreck. Catherine lumbered over to the door, closing it behind her as she went back out into the hallway. The room was dark except for the faint light from the street below. I looked up at the molding on the ceiling, tracing it with my eyes as I did every night before I went to sleep. I followed it around and around, imagining a toy train on the ceiling racing on a track. I heard the wheels of the stretcher again in the hall. I climbed out of bed, snuck over to the door, and peeked out.

Even half-dead, Mother was beautiful. She had the icy good looks of a Hitchcock heroine—a high forehead, long, thin nose, and striking cheekbones. Her blond hair, most of which was a fall attached to the top of her head and expertly teased to create a tumbling-mane effect, lay tousled on the stretcher pillow. She was wearing her blue Pucci peignoir set that brought out the color of her eyes—which were now, of course, closed.

My chest felt twisty as I watched the men in white uniforms with blue jackets wheel her down the hallway and out of the apartment. I believed Mother was safe with the calm, quiet stretcher men and their nicely combed hair and cast-down eyes, but I wondered where they were they taking her, and what they would do. Did they have some magic way of waking her up—a special drink, true love's kiss? Would they put her in a glass box like Snow White while she slept? I felt anxious as the questions kept coming. How long would she be gone? What would I tell my sister?

I climbed back into bed and stared again at the ceiling, trying to slow my racing mind. The low murmuring of my stepfather and the firemen ended with the clicking of the lock of the front door, and a quiet stillness came down. I was left alone with my thoughts, listening to my sister's soft breathing. I squeezed my eyes shut and rolled over, pulling the blanket carefully over my neck so that if Barnabas Collins, the vampire in my favorite TV show, *Dark Shadows*, somehow got into my room, he couldn't bite me there.

As I slept, Mother was swept off to Bellevue Hospital in an ambulance. At the hospital they pumped all the Seconal out of her and kept her for psychiatric evaluation for twenty-four hours, which, we were to discover later, was about ten thousand hours too short. By the time she was released into my stepfather's care, he had already paid off the hospital officials to keep her name out of their records and his name out of the papers: she was never there, it never happened.

The next morning, my sister and I got up and got dressed for school, putting on our dark blue jumpers and pulling on our navy kneesocks. It seemed like any other morning until we walked down the hallway past our mother's now open door and our shoes crunched on the broken glass as I realized it hadn't been a dream.

"Where's Mommy?" my sister asked, peering into Mother's empty bedroom.

As the older child (I was nine) and a witness to the previous night's events, I felt I should provide some sort of explanation about just where our mother might be, even though I didn't really know. I decided to make it into a kind of game, so Robbie wouldn't feel afraid or think that I was worried.

"She went away last night with Pop," I told her. "She

rode away with Pop in a bed on wheels," I added, hoping this would sound like something fun, like a ride at an amusement park.

Robin considered this but didn't say anything, so I figured it sounded pretty good. Even at nine, I was quickly learning how to extemporaneously compose an alibi for Mother.

In the kitchen, Catherine had prepared our breakfast of fried bologna, which she liked to remind us was a great delicacy in her country, Trinidad. I didn't like bologna, but I was hungry so I ate it.

"Mommy's gone," Robin told Catherine.

Catherine, her big horn-rimmed glasses steamy from the stove, pushed more bologna around in the pan and then buttered some toast. "I know, honey," she said. "Your momma has gone to have a little rest. Sometimes, mommas get so tired."

What Catherine was probably thinking was that she didn't have a clue why my mother was so tired since she never did a lick of work and smoked too much.

"What's bologna made out of, anyway?" I asked.

"She's like a flower, your momma," Catherine continued, as if she hadn't heard me. "When she comes home, you girls be quiet and tiptoe around for a while, till she feels strong again."

"We will," I promised.

"So damn skinny," I heard Catherine mutter under her breath as we ran off to get our coats for school.

In the foyer, Catherine rebuttoned my sister's lopsided cardigan and then bundled us into our navy blue coats, carefully pulling mittens over our hands and wrapping scarves around our necks. Having safely stuffed us into our winter wear, she opened the door to the landing and gave us each a gentle push out the door.

"Have a good day at school, now," she called out.

The elevator man took us downstairs and we walked through the large cobblestone courtyard to the iron gates that led out onto Seventy-second Street, where the doorman opened the school bus door for us, tipping his hat to the driver.

Catherine watched us and gave a little wave from the window like she did every day—a promise that she would be there waiting for us. No matter what happened, Catherine held down the fort, striving to instill structure and a sense of normalcy in our lives. This was her quest.

As soon as we were safely on the bus, she returned to the kitchen to start cooking up a batch of her special syrup. She put a pot on the stove and started juicing lemons and limes and chopping up fresh ginger. Then she added honey and cayenne pepper. The special syrup that she made was her answer for almost any ailment. If you had a cold, if you couldn't sleep, if you had a scraped knee, the syrup was just what you needed. And whether she fed it to our mother or rubbed it on her chest, Catherine honestly believed it would restore my mother's body and soul. It would fatten her up and make her stop acting so crazy.

When we came home from school, Mother was still not home. "A few more days," Catherine said when we looked up at her expectantly. "Go have a snack in the kitchen," she said as she unfastened our coats. After dinner, she put us in the bathtub, where we splashed and played while she sat on top of the toilet and laughed at us, covering her teeth with her hand.

"You two are so silly. Find the soap and wash up before you get pruney." Catherine heaved herself up and took the towels off the rack. When we were washed, she wrapped us up like mummies and vigorously rubbed our backs to make us warm.

Then we put on our nighties and followed her as she padded back to her room, behind the kitchen. Robbie and I climbed up on the soft, camel-colored blanket on her twin bed and watched *I Dream of Jeannie* on the little black-and-white TV that sat on her bureau. Catherine sat in an armchair near the bed, laughing at the blond lady on the show and playing with the gold necklace she wore around her neck with a Jesus pendant that was usually wedged between her big bosoms. This was one of my favorite parts of the day. Even when Mother was home, she was usually out, and the apartment was like a maze of empty, chilly rooms, your footsteps echoing up to the high ceilings. Catherine's room was small but warm and we were all together.

When TV time was over, we went to bed. "Good night, my lambie pies," Catherine said as she tucked us into our bunks, kissing us on our foreheads.

After Mother's return from Bellevue, she was silent and gloomy. She wasn't awake when we left for school. In the afternoons, we'd find her to kiss her hello. And then at supper, after finishing our homework, we'd eat and she would smoke and finish what was left of a bottle of Pouilly-Fuissé she'd opened at five.

If Mother's plan with her suicide attempt had been to lure my stepfather back to make him regret what he was about to lose, it hadn't worked. He stayed at the Carlyle and she stayed on the Upper West Side, wandering about the apartment like a beautiful animal at the zoo. She paced the long corridors and grand rooms: the library, where the Rodin sculpture was set against a massive wall of books; the dining room, with its long, white marble table and the low-hanging, heavy sterling chandelier that almost touched it; the butler's pantry, behind a swinging, leather-clad door, its glass cabinets stocked with china and crystal emblazoned with R for "Rea."

And then one day, she was better. We came home from school to find her smiling and pacing up and down the main hall with her cigarette, directing the men who were measuring our furniture and estimating the number of boxes needed to pack everything up. We were moving, she announced, to Park Avenue.

"Is it far? Do we have to go to a new school?" Robbie asked, looking confused.

"No, darling, it's just across town on the Upper East Side. It's actually closer to your school," Mother said, smiling.

"Yeah!" Robbie and I both jumped up and down, clapping. Mother was happy and everything was going to be fine.

That day, Mother gave Catherine the night off and even fixed dinner for us, and we all ate together in the kitchen.

"Now go get ready for bedtime, girls."

Robbie and I looked at each other and hurried down the hall before Mother could change her mind. Mother rarely put us to bed herself, so this counted as a special event. We were all snuggled in our bunks, faces washed, teeth brushed, when Mother sat down in the corner rocking chair, where Catherine usually sat, and told us a bedtime story.

"Once upon a time," she began, "there was a little girl named Loretta who had been left in an orphanage."

Oh, goody, I thought, *like the little girl in* The Secret Garden, *one of my favorite books.*

"And she was me."

I blinked and glanced down at Robbie. This was a true story? Wide-eyed, she looked back at me with surprise.

Mother explained that Loretta was her name before she was adopted. Her birth parents had a drunken quarrel on a bridge one night somewhere in Iowa, and her father tried to throw her mother off the bridge. He was arrested. Before he got out of jail, perhaps to finish the job, her mother dumped all four of their children in an orphanage on her way out of town and disappeared. Mother was two years old at the time. "I remember sitting on the floor of the orphanage, crying and crying. I felt so lonely. And I missed my mommy and daddy and brothers and sister. I used to sit in the corner all day singing, 'Nobody loves me, everybody hates me, I think I'll go eat worms.'"

"Eeeew," my sister said.

"Ssshh," I hushed her, not wanting to miss any of the details.

"Then one day a man and a woman came and saw me. The man was tall and thin. The woman was short and fat. They thought I was such a pretty little girl, with big blue eyes and curly blond hair, that they decided to take me home. You see, they were sad they couldn't have any children of their own."

Just like the couple in The Gingerbread Boy, I thought.

"They scooped me up and took me home! I still remember that day I drove away in the car with my new parents. I waved good-bye to the nuns and thought about how lucky I was that I had been chosen from all the other children," Mother said wistfully.

Bill and Bertha McAdams adopted Mother, changed her name from Loretta (too white trash) to Georgann, and took her home to live in their nice house in the lovely Plaza section of Kansas City, Missouri.

It was strange for me to imagine Mother as a little girl and having a different name. Closing my eyes, I tried to picture it. The truth is that my mother would have been better off staying in the orphanage.

"When we got home, she beat me with a belt buckle because I had forgotten to go to the bathroom before our car trip and we had had to stop. You can still see the scars on my legs."

Behind the quiet shade trees, wide green lawn, and impressive colonial brick façade of Mother's new home, abuse would be doled out daily by her new mother, while her new father spent his days in the hushed offices of his bank. As far as he was concerned, the house and the raising of children were his wife's business, and she insured his ignorance by threatening Georgann with even worse if she complained to him.

"Many years went by. And then, when I was about sixteen, your grandmother wanted me to go with her to the basement to clean up some mess down there that she thought I'd made."

When Mother told stories about the horrible Bertha, her eyes got all glassy and her voice small and simple like a little kid's. "So I followed her to the door of the basement and she started down the stairs," said Mother.

I knew the stairs she meant; they were in my grandfather's house in Kansas City. I had climbed up and down them with my sister. They were dark and steep, and the basement air was damp and smelled of Listerine, mothballs, and the sticky residue of old electrical tape.

"I stood there looking down at the back of her head and thought about the time she'd broken my arm and sent me to school."

Mother fainted in her classroom at school a few days later from the pain. At the hospital they had to break her arm again to set it so it would heal properly.

"I thought about the time I got my red velvet dress dirty

before a party, and she took a pair of scissors and cut it to ribbons."

Bertha made my mother wear the tattered dress to school the next day.

"I looked at her big back going down the stairs in front of me and I suddenly had this impulse to kill her."

I opened my eyes wide and stared at the plaster molding on the ceiling, no longer wanting to see the story in my head. I wished she would stop telling it.

"No one would ever know that she hadn't just fallen; she was so fat. I followed her down the stairs, which creaked underneath her. I held on to the railings on either side of the stairs"—Mother grasped the arms of her chair—"and raised myself up off the ground."

Robin and I watched Mother as she lifted herself lightly out of the chair to reenact the scene.

"I bent my knees and pointed my feet right at her."

Hovering above the chair, Mother lifted one foot off the floor and karate-kicked the air.

"If I kicked her with all my strength, she'd go tumbling down the steps and break her neck." Mother hung there suspended for a moment and thought of the crimes this woman had committed: the beatings, the broken bones, the humiliations, the cruelties doled out every day like multivitamins.

"I wanted her to die for everything she did. But something stopped me." Mother lowered herself back into the chair.

"I thought, 'No, I'll wait. Her time will come.'" Mother relaxed back into the chair and slowly folded her arms across her chest. One corner of her mouth curled up into a small smile.

"I didn't have to wait too long either . . . about two years. She was dying slowly from cancer. No one told her she was sick. Back then they thought it was bad for a patient to know. But I knew. I was eighteen and the doctors thought I was old enough.

"I watched that wicked old woman being taken from the house on a stretcher, her body eaten up with disease, and I knew she was never coming back. 'You just wait till I get home! I'll fix you!' she just kept screaming at me."

By this time Bertha was out of her mind on morphine and had just a few days to live. Mother smiled and waved, watching Bertha being put in the ambulance, knowing that her mother would never touch her again and would burn in some special circle of hell for everything she had done.

"After she died, my daddy came to me and asked me to pick out a dress for my mother to be buried in. 'Of course I will, Daddy. You go rest now, you've been through so much,' I said.

Mother drove downtown to the fancy shops on the Plaza and bought the perfect dress for Bertha to wear for her eternal rest—black with little pink flowers and pink trim.

"You see, pink had always been Bertha's least favorite color and now she would have to wear it for the rest of time."

Mother folded her hands in her lap and smiled at us from the chair, triumphant.

She'd got her happy ending. And we'd just got a taste of the Brothers Grimm by way of Kansas City.

Sweet dreams . . .

chapter two

RUNAWAY BRIDE

Because Georgann had been so brave during Bertha's horrific illness and lingering subsequent death, my grandfather decided to buy her a new car. It seemed like the least he could do after she had lost her mother at such a young age, especially since she had been so strong and such a help to him. He took her downtown and bought her a red-and-white Buick Riviera for her very own. Emotions were not his strong suit, so buying her the Buick was easier than telling her how much he loved her, and how sorry he was for everything she had been through. He was satisfied when he saw how happy she was behind the wheel of her new, fancy automobile.

My grandfather may have missed Bertha, but saw no reason to grieve. Life went on and he never looked back—not at the home he ran away from in Appalachia at fourteen, not at his pals who were killed fighting beside him against

Pancho Villa, not at the mahogany coffin in which they lowered Bertha into the ground. He threw his handful of dirt into the grave and walked away.

Despite the death of her nemesis and having a new car, Georgann was hopelessly unhappy. The absence of Bertha had not made her father less remote or her cosseted life any less confining; she felt hollow inside. She returned to school and poured herself into writing poetry, frantically searching for something to fill up the emptiness and make her feel loved and important.

It wasn't long before my poor father stumbled unknowingly into Mother's field of vision and got caught in the crosshairs of her desperation. Their marriage lasted seven years—the first of which may have been happy . . . until they got to know each other better.

My father, James Lawless, was born in a small town called Brockville in Ontario, Canada. He was the oldest of five children. His father owned a small dental laboratory and spent his days making false teeth. His mother was an Irish Catholic housewife who attended church daily and lived in her kitchen, cooking bacon and drinking endless cups of tea. My father never saw his parents display any physical affection for each other, no kisses or hugs. Any intimacy between them must have occurred behind closed doors—at least five times. The rest of the time my grandfather Lawless preferred his drinking buddies and his cigars, while my grandmother favored fussing over her children and saying the rosary. At school, the nuns tied my father's left arm behind his back to force him to become right-handed—everyone knew that left-handed people had the devil inside—but he stayed a lefty despite their efforts. When they forced him to be in the school play as part of his detention, he discovered Shakespeare and was immediately enthralled by its all-consuming beauty, humor, and passion. He became head of the drama club and won many awards for his acting. Standing onstage, beneath the hot, bright lights, reciting fiery prose—he realized there was more to the world than the gray, lifeless winters at home.

Eventually, my father was awarded a scholarship to study theater at the University of Missouri in Kansas City. I have a photograph of him from this time; he was tall and gangly with a head of dark hair and enormous blue eyes. When I would ask Mother why she married him, she would take a long drag on her cigarette and say, "It was those eyes of his, those damn cow eyes." He had long black lashes, and his eyes were always slightly watery, which made them look dreamy and full of emotion.

My mother first saw my father in a play at the university in Kansas City and said to her girlfriend Sylvia, "I am going to marry that man." Sylvia was my mother's best friend and partner in crime. They had both attended St. Teresa's Academy for young ladies, where they had smoked in the bathroom together and climbed on the ledge outside the science lab on a dare. Mother probably didn't need to announce her intentions to Sylvia, as Sylvia would grow up to be a famous psychic, author, and daytime talk show regular.

Even with her psychic abilities as yet undeveloped, Sylvia knew how determined my mother could be, but nothing could have prepared my father for the full force of the juggernaut heading his way—a desperate, beautiful, poetry-writing blonde, hell-bent on escape.

My parents courted secretly, holding hands at Winstead's, a famous Kansas City hamburger stand that has long outlived their marriage. I can picture them there when they were still happy—sitting at a pink Formica table in a gray-green Naugahyde booth drinking milk shakes, playing the little tabletop jukebox, and staring into each other's eyes. They had to sneak around back then because my grandfather would never have given his blessing to a foreigner—worse, an actor—even if he was Catholic. My grandfather worried that his daughter marrying my father would surely condemn her to destitution or deportation or some equally horrible fate.

But before my father knew what had hit him, he and my mother had eloped and were married by a justice of the peace in Oklahoma. Fearing my grandfather's wrath, they kept the wedding a secret, and my mother returned home after the ceremony wearing her wedding ring around her neck on a chain. My mother was nineteen and my father was twenty-two at the time, but their marriage wasn't discovered for a whole year—until my mother had become pregnant with me and had started to show.

My grandfather was furious but he bought them a house to live in and made them get remarried in a church so he wouldn't be embarrassed in front of his friends. He had always regarded his daughter as a dreamy girl who read too many books; she was flighty and high-strung and now she'd run off with a man who didn't have a real job. *God only knows what will happen,* he thought to himself. At least, thanks to him, they had a roof over their heads.

Marriage wasn't the escape my mother had dreamed it would be. It was a trap in which she was alone all day with an infant (me), dirty dishes and laundry to do, while my father went to his announcer job at a classical radio station. By the time my sister came along fourteen months later, my father knew that my mother was not only deeply troubled but also felt suffocated by her new life as a wife and mother.

The modest house we lived in was a fraction of the size of her parents', with simple wooden furniture bought on layaway and not as nice as she would have liked. There was nothing romantic about it, nothing as beautiful or fulfilling as my mother had been led to believe about marriage in books and movies. And when, in short order, she was pregnant with my sister, my father would come home to find her catatonic on the sofa, with a daiquiri in one hand and a cigarette in the other, while I screamed in my playpen in the corner of the room and the hi-fi belted out Frank Sinatra. She was lonely and disappointed, and even though she told my father so, her unhappiness mystified him.

One day, after my sister was two or three, my father came home from work to discover that my mother had locked us in the hall closet for the day.

"In you go," she had ordered. She held the door open for us and tapped her foot, waiting. Robbie and I walked in; there was nowhere to sit so we sat on the floor, underneath all the winter coats smelling of mothballs and smoke. Mother closed the door and then locked it. A slit of light came from under the door, and slowly our eyes adjusted.

"I'm scared," Robbie said, starting to cry.

"Shhh, if she hears you, she'll come back and be even madder." I reached over and linked my arm through hers.

"It's dark in here," she sniffed.

"Let's pretend we're in the forest at night." I felt along the wall for Daddy's tennis racket and placed it on the floor flat in front of us. "This is our firewood. You make a campfire and I'll look for food to cook." I stood up and fished around in Daddy's winter coat pockets. I found half a roll of Life Savers.

"Candy!" I whispered. It was dark but I could smell that they were wild cherry. I peeled the paper back and gave the first one to Robbie. We shared the roll, sucking quietly in the dark, rubbing our hands together in front of the make-believe fire.

We sang all the songs we knew as softly as we could— "Itsy Bitsy Spider," "Three Blind Mice," "This Old Man," and "Twinkle, Twinkle, Little Star."

"Up above the world so high, like a diamond in the sky . . ."

Finally, I pulled some coats down onto the floor and we

slipped in and out of sleep while we waited for our father to come home and rescue us.

It had been about six hours when I heard Daddy's car coming into the garage alongside the house and then the front door opening and closing. I could hear my parents talking through the door, first quietly, then more loudly. I heard him ask her where we were. Then I heard my father's footsteps striding up to the door, and the key turning in the lock.

He pulled the light-switch cord and looked down at us. "Are you girls all right?" He crouched down on the floor and looked into our faces. His forehead was all wrinkled, and I didn't want to see him look so worried. But I burst into tears along with Robbie, unable to maintain my stoic front any longer. We were so happy to see him, so happy it was over.

"Oh, Daddy." I reached out my hand to him and stood up, then pulled my sister to her feet.

"Daddy, I'm hungry," Robin sobbed, and my father hugged us both close. We rubbed our eyes and squinted from the light the way you do when you come out of a dark movie theater on a sunny day. Then we followed my father into the living room, where Mother was sitting calmly on the sofa reading a magazine.

She went to the hospital the next day.

After Mother had been there for a full week, Daddy took us for a visit. I was excited to see her; it felt like she'd been gone for such a long time. When we pulled into the parking lot, I noticed a few people walking around, but none of them looked sick. I asked my father why no one was in a wheel-chair or wearing a hospital gown, and he told me that it was a special kind of hospital for people who had tired brains.

The hospital was bright and clean inside and smelled like a swimming pool. Mother's room was all bleached white and glowing with sunlight. Her blond hair was pulled back in a bun. Looking at her in the skinny hospital bed, I didn't think she looked sick at all. She looked beautiful, like a fairy princess.

Mother laughed and smiled and was so happy to see us. Daddy stood against the wall with his arms crossed over his chest, as we climbed up onto the bed to hug her and kiss her. She told us that she got to eat her breakfast in bed and that most nights they showed movies in the dining room after dinner. She told us about a woman she'd met there who had been a famous Olympic diver, but then had dived into a swimming pool with no water in it and now she had problems thinking straight. I wondered aloud why someone would jump into an empty swimming pool in the first place, but Mother said it had been an accident.

Before we left, she gave us each a little pair of moc-casins that she had made for us during recreation. I asked what that was, and she said it was a time when everyone at the hospital got to make something with her hands—baskets or pot holders, for example—and that she had decided to make something for us. The moccasins were brown suede and had little beads sewn onto the tops of them—they were so pretty. I told her I loved them. Then a nurse came in and said that visiting hours were over and we kissed Mother good-bye.

"I'll be home soon," she promised.

I rode home in the car smiling the whole way with my moccasins on my lap. I told my father that I planned to wear them to school the next day to show everyone. My father said nothing; he just looked out at the road over the steering wheel.

chapter three

FATAL ATTRACTION

When the classical-music radio station went under, my father took a job acting in summer stock in Chapel Hill, North Carolina. Perhaps he hoped a change of scenery might help improve my mother's frame of mind. She had even been offered a few small speaking parts in the plays. It was only when we arrived that my father learned the actors were to be housed in a nearby trailer park—a fact that may not have thrilled my mother, but she took it on the chin, happy to be out of Kansas City.

The trailer park was built on land donated to the town by a wealthy businessman on the condition that no black people live there or even enter the park that surrounded it. Our parents were the youngest people living there by far; everyone else was old and sat in folding chairs in their yards all day. Our neighbor Sam used to take his teeth out or pretend to steal Robbie's and my noses, but it was really his thumb.

Sam lived with his wife, Gloria, and their collie dog and some chickens they kept.

One day, when we were playing out front, we saw Sam heading to his coop with an ax. He came back carrying a flapping chicken by the legs. He laid it on top of a stump and held it still with the toe of his boot, then he chopped its head off. Robin and I were thrilled and disgusted all at the same time. We had never seen anything killed and couldn't take our eyes off the chicken's severed head, eyes still blinking as it lay in the dirt. Then Sam let go of the chicken's body, and it started running around the yard in a wide circle without its head, to the delight of us all. It was kind of like a cartoon— the chicken running around headless for about a minute before flopping to the ground. Then, as if to extinguish its life completely, Sam's collie leapt forward and gobbled up the head.

Robin and I spent the days running around the trailer park, and the nights in the back of our station wagon in the parking lot of the theater. Since the theater was outdoors, Mother lowered the backseat and made a bed for us with pillows and blankets. We would lie there in our pajamas, and if we got frightened, we only had to sit up to glimpse our parents lit up on the stage.

The little local paper did a story on Mother: young, plucky wife of an actor and mother of two living in summer lodgings, writing poetry, and washing her husband's socks. The article had a picture of Mother sitting on the steps of the trailer with my sister and me, dressed in matching plaid sunsuits, our hair cut pixie-style for summer, on her lap. Perhaps in defiance of the drabness of her surroundings, Mother is wearing a stunning white sheath dress and her hair is in a French-twist updo à la Tippi Hedren in *The Birds*. In the photo, we are all smiling and squinting into the sun. Being featured in the newspaper was Mother's first taste of fame, and she liked it. She liked the compliments on her acting she received at the cast parties, and she liked being the prettiest among the other summer-stock wives. She was a local celebrity, the glamorous wife of a dashing actor.

Mother's happiness made our time in Chapel Hill feel more like one long extended summer vacation. The days were warm and sunny and we were near enough to the ocean to spend our parents' days off there. Mother had never seen the ocean and instantly fell in love. Every Monday, she would pack us a picnic and we'd spend the day in the sun. My father would take Robbie and me down to the water, where we shrieked at the way the sand sucked up our feet, while he skipped stones for us. And Mother would sit on a bedspread we used as a beach blanket and read a book or more often just stare out at the water.

At the end of the summer, when the playhouse closed up for the winter, my father was offered a contract understudying and playing small roles at the Guthrie Theater in Minneapolis. It was a chance to get in on the ground floor of what was promising to be the country's leading regional theater. At my mother's insistence, he took it. She never wanted to go back to her hometown, and her first brush with the spotlight had made her want more. We packed up the station wagon and drove to Minnesota.

To keep my mother occupied and feeling useful in Minneapolis, my father found her a volunteer position at the Guthrie. He thought using her English degree and poetry-writing skills to help with a new translation of Anton Chekhov's *The Three Sisters* would engage her and get her away from the dull routines of the housewife. The translation was being overseen by one of the theater's founders, Oliver Rea. And he was nothing if not engaging.

Oliver Rea was a successful Broadway producer who, disenchanted with the New York theater scene, had moved his family to Minneapolis to found the Guthrie Theater, where he and Sir Tyrone Guthrie, a scion of the English stage, planned to produce serious classical theater. He came from a very wealthy, old-moneyed, socially prominent family—the kind who appear in *Who's Who in America* and the Social Register—and had been raised by nannies on an estate. He had been all over the world, spoke French, wore cologne, smoked Gitanes, and dressed impeccably in clothes that were tailor-made for him. He wasn't handsome but had a craggy allure and an air of mystery that my mother found fatally glamorous. He was also fifteen years her senior and married with three children. Oliver was rumored to have gambled away a million dollars before he was thirty. The first time my mother walked into his office at the theater, she was smitten; he was like a movie star or a character in a book. Mother couldn't resist him. He was everything my father wasn't.

While my father was working with Sir Tyrone, Jessica Tandy, Hume Cronyn, and George Grizzard, my mother began having a raging affair with Oliver Rea. Soon, everyone at the theater knew about it—except my father, who innocently would never have imagined his wife capable of such a thing.

To celebrate the successful season at the Guthrie, Oliver and his wife, Betty, gave a soiree for the entire theater company and staff at their mansion in the fashionable Loring Park section of Minneapolis. They were the sort of people who threw big, fancy parties, effortlessly, all the time, and they did it well. Everyone in town was there, drinking and enjoying hors d'oeuvres around one of the few swimming pools in the Twin Cities.

While my sister and I played in the pool with my future stepfather's children, my father stood out on the flagstone patio with his fellow actor and friend Douglas Campbell. Dougie, a larger-than-life Scotsman, was extolling the charms of an exotically beautiful French costumer who was standing on the other side of the pool surrounded by a throng of men, when my father suddenly realized he hadn't seen his wife since they'd arrived an hour earlier.

All I saw from the pool was my father head for the bar under an awning on the other side of the patio and refresh his drink before going inside. Apparently, after winding his way through all the imposing rooms downstairs, aggressively decorated in the old-money manner of Sister Parish with lots of chintz and antiques, my father climbed the stairs, ice cubes clinking in his glass, to locate his wife.

When my father got to the top of the landing, he heard loud voices, one of them my mother's, coming from behind a closed bedroom door. He opened the door and walked in. Oliver and my mother were standing very close together, and he had his hands locked on my mother's wrists. He let go of her and they quickly sprang apart. Completely bewildered, my father asked, "What the hell's going on here?" My mother walked wordlessly past him and Oliver followed. Then, perhaps emboldened by the discovery of their secret, the lovers walked down the stairs holding hands to where the party was in full swing.

Mother cleared her throat dramatically. "Ladies and gentlemen, we have an announcement to make." She looked rapturously at my stepfather, and it was then that my father knew what was so horribly true. "Oliver Rea and I are in love." Mother moved close to him and took his arm.

"We are leaving here together," my future stepfather said, gazing into Mother's eyes.

Everybody froze mid-canapé with a scotch stuck to their hands and their mouths hanging open. Oliver and my mother glided past this frozen tableau. My father followed them outside, speechless, and watched as the lovers got into a Jag and drove off. Betty ran out of the house and up to my father. They stood there together on the sidewalk, like fire victims watching their home burn as the car disappeared into the night.

My father turned to Betty and asked, "Did you know about this?"

"Yes," she answered with the world-weariness of a woman who knows her husband has chased most of her girlfriends around the coffee table and caught quite a few. "This has happened before. But," she said, maybe to reassure my father and herself, "he always comes back."

My father then noticed that Betty was trembling and soaking wet. He took off his coat and wrapped it tightly around her. As they walked back to the house, she told him about the little blond girl who had started to drown in the pool.

"I'm not much of a swimmer but I jumped in. She had sunk like a stone to the bottom of the pool, poor thing. That's where I was when all this happened."

My father ran through the house to the patio, where he found my sister, bundled up in blankets on a chaise by the pool, her teeth chattering, her lips blue.

Like all the other kids, I'd been having fun and was oblivious to what was happening until I saw the dark flash of a fully dressed woman jumping into the water. After Robbie was safely out of the pool, I stood there next to her, holding her ice-cold hand, both of us in a kind of shock to be surrounded by a crowd of people. When my father rushed up, I watched his face shift from bewildered dread to relief as he saw my sister, grabbed her, and hugged her.

Daddy, Robbie, and I were eating hot dogs and baked beans around the kitchen table when the phone rang. He was still in full makeup from the matinee of *Richard III*, and I remember how strange it looked to see him answer. It was my mother. The public announcement of the affair and the uproar it had produced caused her to suffer another nervous breakdown, and she had checked into a hospital to "rest."

She told my father that she was sorry about all of it, and she wanted to come back home. The affair was over and she begged my father to forgive her. She had been so bored, so lonely—she had even warned my father that something like this might happen if he left her alone too much. So in a way it was partly his fault for being at the theater day and night.

Daddy, although understandably shell-shocked, agreed to take her back, thinking it was best for Robbie and me to have a mother even if she was unbalanced and a faithless liar. This was the way people thought in the sixties—a mother, even a lousy one, was better than no mother at all. Parents stayed together for the sake of the children back then; his own mother and father had remained in their loveless marriage for the same reason. And so he forgave her. Mother told him she was tired of weaving baskets and making those goddamn pot holders in the recreational therapy room and could he bring her typewriter to the hospital the next day. Sure, he said, and he hung up.

The next day, we all drove to the hospital to see Mother and bring her the typewriter, but she was gone.

"She checked out with her husband," the nurse said, looking at my dad like he was as screwy as everyone else in the place. My sister and I looked down the empty hallways of the hospital, smelling the familiar medicinal chlorine odor.

"But I'm her husband," he yelled at her. Robbie and I sought each other's hands.

Mother had made a break for freedom, and if she planned to do any writing, it would have to be with a pen.

A week later, a postcard arrived from the Caribbean. In my mother's curly, perfect Catholic-school handwriting she wrote that she was there with my stepfather, she wanted a divorce, and that the weather was warm and sunny.

Mother still had not returned when Daddy told us to sit on the sofa. He knelt in front of us and explained that Mother had decided to marry someone else. He said it was a good thing because it would make her happy. He told us the most important thing to remember was that he loved us and nothing would ever change that.

"But who are you going to marry?" I asked. I didn't want him to be alone.

"No one right now, okay?"

I nodded and felt the saddest I had ever felt, my eyes burning with tears. Robbie said nothing but buried her face in my shoulder, most likely trying to block out what our father was telling us.

"You are going to go live in New York with your mother, and I'm going to stay here."

I bit my lip and looked down at my hands.

"But when will we see you?" asked Robbie, her voice muffled by tears and my sweater.

"Every summer, I promise." Then Daddy gathered us in his arms and kissed us. Holding onto his neck, I smelled the starch on his shirt collar and numbly realized that there was nothing I could do to stop this from happening.

Mother returned from the Caribbean, and my step-father-to-be swept us all off to Manhattan. Daddy got his own two-bedroom apartment near the Guthrie. Once the divorces were final, my mother and stepfather were married in the apartment in the Dakota, which was his wedding present to her.

On the morning of the wedding, Robin and I were summoned to Mother's room to show her the new white dresses with lace trim she had chosen for us to wear to the ceremony. I held my breath, hoping we would pass inspection. Mother was sitting at her vanity table in front of her Clairol light-up mirror in a white silk bra, pearls, and a half-slip. She was teasing her hair, which was a good six inches above her scalp, making her look as though she'd been electrocuted.

"Let me look at you." She twirled her comb in the air as we turned in a circle.

"Good Lord, Robin, come here and let me brush your hair. It looks like chicken feathers."

My little sister always had a look of dishevelment. Her flyaway hair and a big gap between her two front teeth made her look as if she'd been running backward through the briar patch. She usually had food on her face and looked slightly guilty, like she'd been playing with matches. She was a slob. I, on the other hand, always looked like the little girl in the

Breck shampoo commercial. My blond hair was smooth and shiny, my teeth were straight, and I never had chocolate on my face or dirty fingernails. Robbie was seemingly untouched by the prospect of Mother's disapproval, whereas I constantly sought to avoid it. I accepted the job of protecting Robbie as a part of my role as flawless older sister. The differences between us could have been a source of conflict in our relationship, but they weren't. It was clear even then that being Miss Perfect never gained me any points.

If Robbie's crime was lack of grooming, mine was looking just like my father. "You look just like your father," Mother would say, making her eyes all small and mean looking.

"Ouch!" Robbie winced as Mother attempted to tame her wild-child hair.

"All right, that's better."

Mother leaned toward us, opened her arms, and drew us to her. She smelled like her new perfume, which was very sweet and expensive. It even had a name that went with her new life: Joy.

"You are both very pretty." Mother turned back to her mirror to finish her hair.

"Are we really?" I asked.

"Well, of course you are—if you hadn't been pretty, I would have given you away," she said casually, lacquering her bouffant with Final Net.

My sister and I looked at her, confused. Mother caught a glimpse of our perplexed faces in the mirror and smiled. "You sillies, it's just an expression." She laughed, shaking her comb at us as if it were a magic wand. "Now run along and don't get dirty."

"Yes, ma'am." Blushing with happiness that we had pleased our mother, Robbie and I went out into the foyer to practice our handshakes and curtsies with the wedding guests as Mother had taught us.

My mother and stepfather were married in front of the mantelpiece in the living room by a man in a long black dress who must have been someone who officiated at the weddings of people who had been married before. Mother looked radiant in a chic Oleg Cassini suit of robin's-egg blue. Her blond hair shone like Grace Kelly's and her beauty lit up the room. She smiled as my stepfather slid three Cartier bands on her finger—she hadn't been able to decide which one she liked best so, of course, he bought them all.

It must have seemed to my mother as if she had finally realized the life she had dreamed about when she planned her escape from Kansas City. A million-dollar apartment in New York, servants, shows, nightclubs, shopping, and lunches with the beautiful and wealthy. But, after plucking Mother from her life as a Midwestern housewife, dressing her up at Bergdorf's, and surrounding her with elegant things, my stepfather took off. I never knew if it was to work, to drink, or to screw—probably all three—but his intent was definitely not to squire her around.

Once again, as in her first marriage, she was alone. The apartment in the Dakota was just a more glamorous cage to be locked in, along with the rest of my stepfather's possessions: his autographed first editions, his cavalry sword from military school, and the signed photo of his flight instructor, Charles Lindbergh.

Mother started sleeping during the day and walking the halls of the apartment at night in a diaphanous, white Dior negligee, smoking, with a glass of something on the rocks in her hand, trying to figure out how to lure my stepfather home.

She tried threatening divorce and he accepted. She tried suicide and he called her bluff. It was time to fold and call her lawyer.

chapter four

THE LOVE CHILD

After their Mexican divorce, and per her plan, my step-father sold my mother the apartment in the Dakota for one dollar. She in turn sold it for a lot more and moved us and Catherine to what my mother perceived as a more fashionable side of town.

Our apartment at 1192 Park Avenue was smaller than the one in the Dakota (four bedrooms instead of six), but it was no less fancy. Fortuny silk still covered the furniture, signed first editions of Hemingway and Faulkner still graced the shelves, and the black Steinway still sat in front of the living room windows, unplayed. What did have to change when we moved was Robbie and me. Mother was now a rich Upper East Side divorcée and she required children to match. From the day we moved east, Robin and I were always dressed impeccably and often identically in Florence Eiseman dresses and patent leather shoes. We looked like all the other sophisticated little girls in New York who attended private school, visited the Metropolitan Museum of Art and the Natural History Museum at least twice a year, and ate at Schrafft's with their nannies on Saturday afternoons after seeing a movie at Radio City Music Hall or taking ice-skating lessons at Rockefeller Center. We were adorable. And even when we were miserable, we were miserable in the right clothes in all the right places. That was what mattered to my mother.

Once word got out that Mother was newly single and on the market, the boyfriends started to queue up, and Catherine always seemed to be ambling over to answer the front door, smoothing the apron on her new light gray uniform Mother had made her start wearing.

There was Peter Janover, the diminutive rich boy who liked to date women taller than him and wrote down every penny he spent in a little notebook. Then there was Henry Wolf, a successful Madison Avenue advertising man whom I prayed Mother wouldn't marry because then my name would be Wendy Wolf. There was Herb Sargent, a TV writer who used to calmly roll down the cab window and toss Mother's cigarettes out into the street. "Jesus Christ, Herb!" Mother would screech, her aggravation making it so much more entertaining for Robbie and me—we thought Herb was hilarious. There was Joachim Uribe, whom Mother called "that crazy Mexican." He wore a wedding ring, had a hairy back, and owned a gun. And there was Claudia Costa, a sort of Brazilian Ava Gardner who had a love child our age named Lita, with a guy in the Mafia.

Claudia shared my mother's bed one summer in a rented house in Pound Ridge—except when Claudia's lover came to visit, of course. We loved his visits because he would bring Lita a huge Steiff stuffed animal so big we could ride it. He had once been a dancer and could jump up in the air and turn somersaults from a standing position like one of those windup monkeys. He always did it right before our bedtime; he would jump up in the air and turn completely head over heels backward wearing a business suit. I remember the whack of his shiny shoes on the floor when he landed. We girls would clap wildly and jump up and down. Years later he was found dead by the side of the road somewhere in the Midwest, shot in the head. By that time Claudia had disappeared—it was rumored that she had taken Lita and gone to Switzerland.

These were giddy times during which the doorbell was always ringing and the flowers and the gifts never stopped arriving. We rode around in limousines and taxis late at night, looking out at the lights of Manhattan on our way home from dinner or from seeing a Broadway show. Catherine would put us to bed and we would fall asleep listening to Astrud Gilberto records playing over the low din of conversation in the living room. In the morning, we'd wake up and graze last night's party hors d'oeuvres for breakfast. Day-old clams casino was not tasty, but Brie was easy to spread, delicious, and could, in a pinch, be eaten with your fingers. Catherine did not approve, but the evenings ended too late for her to clean up then, and there was too much to do getting us off to school for her to tackle the overflowing ashtrays and souring cocktail glasses before we awoke. But despite her clucking over our preference for French cheese over fried bologna, and extra conflicts over our late nights and heel-dragging in the mornings, Catherine remained our much-loved anchor in the whirlwind of Mother's new life. Her strictness and resolve to provide some kind of structure made us chafe, but drew us closer to her.

On Saturdays that winter, Catherine took us down to Rockefeller Center for our ice-skating lessons. She'd take us into the dressing room and help us put on our skates, using the big lacing hook that she'd pull out of her battered but voluminous black handbag. Catherine's purse was like Mary Poppins's carpetbag. We were constantly surprised by its contents, which she always presented with such nonchalance: a seemingly endless supply of dainty, embroidered hankies, little boxes of raisins, a small, collapsible drinking cup, a flashlight for seeing in a dark movie theater, a sewing kit, and a big whistle on a chain.

"I've never seen anything so crazy," she said, leaning over and grunting as she threaded our skates. "People running around on a floor that's frozen." She laughed and shook her head at the foolishness of it all.

"Thank you, Catherine," Robbie and I both said, as she slowly raised herself up and stashed the hook back in her purse for next time.

"I'll go wait in the restaurant, you two go to Miss Yvonne."

Miss Yvonne was our skating teacher. She was Austrian

and had once been in the Olympics, but now in her dotage was reduced to teaching little rich children. She always wore a short skirt and a pom-pom hat like Sonja Henie in the movies and was overly cheerful in a clipped way that made Robbie and me a bit nervous.

"*Und* now, time for skating!" Miss Yvonne announced at the start of every lesson, clapping her hands up in the air like a Spanish dancer.

Catherine always sat inside the café that looked out on the rink, drinking a cup of Lipton tea, which was her favorite. She watched us while she sipped her tea, waving periodically. Afterward, in the dressing room, she rubbed our frozen feet, trying to warm them up, as we shivered.

"Did you see me?" Robbie and I both asked, even though we knew she had been watching us the whole time.

"What do you think—of course I did! Both of you looked like little dancing snowflakes!" she chuckled.

"Really?"

"Yes, lamb. Now your momma gave me money for a taxi, so hurry and put on your shoes."

We rode home in a cab, sitting on either side of Catherine with our faces against her coat, drowsing while the city went by, happy and warm.

With a Park Avenue address, plenty of money, and her freedom, Mother had become a New York socialite. She was not, and could never be, a member of Mrs. Astor's old-moneyed

Four Hundred, but was a part of the modern, more democratic "society" formed at the confluence of new money, liberal politics, and the arts described by Tom Wolfe as the Radical Chic. In addition to dating, drinking, and partying in all the most fashionable places, Mother and her girlfriends were to be found drinking and partying for all the most fashionable causes—campaigning for John Lindsay, visiting the leftist Puerto Rican Young Lords in their East Harlem stronghold, and raising money for world peace at Yoko Ono's latest performance. None of them would know by looking at Mother's Pucci pantsuit and blond flip hairdo that she had been living in a trailer park only a few years before with people who killed their own chickens for dinner. That was another world, a world my sister and I got to return to in the summers when we went to stay with our father in Minneapolis.

Although we were apart for nine or ten months at a time, Daddy sent us letters, and sometimes cassettes of him talking about his day at the theater. Listening to his deep, velvety voice, we imagined him in his apartment, sitting in the scratchy plaid armchair near the bookcase, drinking a beer in his white Fruit of the Loom undershirt after work—the edges of his face tinged here and there with makeup the cold cream failed to reach. Closing our eyes, we wished ourselves there, next to him.

Though we grew accustomed to our lives as children of the privileged Upper East Side and enjoyed many of its perks, in late spring we would begin to count down the days until we could kick off our party shoes, get to wear jeans, and go to Minneapolis. At the end of June, we'd get off the plane and Daddy would take one look at us in our fancy frocks and Mary Janes and take us straight to Dayton's department store (where Mary Tyler Moore throws up her beret in the introduction to *The Mary Tyler Moore Show*) to buy us play clothes: Danskin shorts and tops, and Garanimals. It was sort of a crazy version of *The Sound of Music* in which the roles were reversed. My father played Maria and saw kids who needed to have some fun, and my mother was Captain von Trapp, worried about our appearance in case the baroness stopped by for tea, or in Mother's case, a vodka gimlet.

In Minneapolis, my sister and I would spend all day outside in our play clothes, never wearing shoes. We would bomb around with a big pack of kids, riding bikes and playing games of red rover or capture the flag that sometimes went on all day. We had a babysitter, always a teenage girl who would inevitably develop a crush on Daddy as the summer progressed, who watched us when he had rehearsals during the day and performances at night.

Once the play was open, his days were free and he spent them with us. We went swimming in Lake Calhoun, to the movies, or sometimes out to eat at the Lincoln Del, our favorite restaurant, which had spaghetti with huge meatballs that we adored.

Daddy was always clowning, making us laugh while he feverishly conducted to Beethoven blasting on the car radio, or driving a hundred miles an hour while we screamed and rolled around giggling on the backseat. Every night before he went to work, we scratched his back and he would grimace and grunt like we were hurting him, even though Robbie and I both knew he loved it.

Sometimes he would take us to the theater with him and we would hang around the greenroom, playing pool and bumming money off the actors to buy snacks from the vending machines. I loved the smell of the theater: an intoxicating perfume of coffee, paint, and wood that to me smelled like romance, beauty, and possibility. I felt about the theater the way Holly Golightly did about Tiffany's—nothing very bad could happen to you there.

At the end of the summer, Robbie and I would tearfully call Mother and beg her to let us stay in Minneapolis with our dad. Mother would listen to us sobbing into the receiver and then ask that we put our father on the line. They exchanged a few words, Mother reiterating the terms of their divorce agreement, and Daddy looking down at the floor, frowning slightly as he listened to my mother tell him we had to return to her.

"I'm sorry, girls," he would say, then carefully and deliberately pack our suitcases himself and put us back on the plane to New York. He always stood at the window of the terminal, waving and smiling, until we took off. I could see the little, dark speck of his head through the small fishbowl window as the plane lifted off the ground and my sister and I cried our eyes out. The flight attendant would come down the aisle and pin on our little gold wings, the accessory of the traveling child of divorce. They were meant to make you feel special but only made you feel even more alone and pathetic. What we really needed was some Kleenex and a hug. At least we had each other—another small hand to hold as the plane rose into the air and the other passengers stared at us, shaking their heads and wondering who would let two little girls fly alone.

The annual ritual ended in New York when my mother would unpack our suitcases and, without skipping a beat, throw out all our play clothes. Those polyester separates just didn't fit in with our cosmopolitan lifestyle. Eloise didn't wear Garanimals to the Plaza for tea, or to her French lesson. Of course, by throwing the clothes away, she cast aside our summer, our time with our father, and our memories, as well as her own. She did not want to be reminded of a time when she'd eaten three-bean salad and certainly not that she had liked it.

The Christmas I was ten, Daddy came to New York to tell us he was planning to marry our stepmother in the summer. We had only met her a couple of times, but I was glad about it. She was the opposite of my mother; not a fair and fragile beauty but handsome and tall with a big, low laugh that made you want to go sit next to her. She looked like the actress Patricia Neal and had three children, whom she had raised on her own as a working mother. I thought it was a wonderful Christmas surprise.

After he told us, Robbie and I ran to the tree in the living room to open our gifts. Daddy had brought us dolls that were dressed like angels, with long gold dresses and starry halos in their blond ringlets. We hung around his neck kissing him while he made funny groaning noises and said we were going to break his back.

"Excuse me," Mother said. "You girls have received other presents, you know." In our Christmas-morning frenzy, we had run right past the gift Mother had given us: an ice cream soda fountain from FAO Schwarz that was so big it couldn't be wrapped. It had red swivel stools, and the white counter had ice cream cones painted on it.

Carrying our dolls, we obediently went over to our mother to thank her for her present. She was wearing a long-sleeved, black wool dress, with her hair pulled back into a severe ponytail, and her face looked all tight. I realized our mistake in not thanking her first, but it also occurred to me that she was not pleased with Daddy's plan to remarry. Looking back later, I think she'd thought my father had traveled to New York to ask her to come back to him, not to announce his engagement to someone else. After breakfast, Mother stood next to the front door with a frozen smile on her face seeing my father out.

"I'll send tickets for the girls," he promised.

"Sure. Great. Good-bye, Jim." Mother shut the door.

My sister and I ran to our bedroom and waved to him from the window when he appeared on the sidewalk below. It was raining and he had turned up the collar of his overcoat. Daddy waved up at us and then popped into a cab and was gone. We watched the taxi drive down Park Avenue.

"And have you had a merry Christmas?" Mother was standing in the doorway, holding two large, black trash bags. She spoke in a quiet, calm tone, but her clenched teeth gave me pause—this had to be a trick question.

"Yes, ma'am." I took Robbie's hand and waited for it to come.

"I want you to each take one of these." She snapped the bags in the air, opening them with a violent crack. We each obediently took one. "You are to put all your old toys and your Christmas presents in these bags, including the one gift your father was kind enough to bring you. They will all be given away to children who deserve them." Mother turned on her heel and started to leave the room.

"But why?" I asked, as Robin started to cry.

"Why?" Mother turned and looked at me, her eyes burning with anger. "Because you don't appreciate anything you have." Her voice grew louder and quavered slightly. Robbie and I instinctively took a step back.

"Did we do something wrong?" I didn't understand what was happening, why she was so furious at us.

"Just put your toys in the bags." She marched out of the room and slammed the door behind her. Terrified and sobbing, Robbie and I started taking our dolls, puzzles, and stuffed animals off the shelves and dropping them into the bags. We hid our favorites—which included the two angel dolls our father had just given us, my sister's teddy bear,

Guthrie, and my Raggedy Andy—on top of the high book-shelf, which you could climb up like a ladder because it was built into the wall. Everything else, including our Christmas presents, went into the trash bags, and we were sent to bed with no dinner.

In the morning, Mother's black mood was gone. She greeted us at breakfast as if nothing had happened. Robbie and I were confused. It was almost as if it had been a dream. Only the absence of our toys, the garbage bags, and the soda fountain told us it wasn't.

Spring came and my mother started to talk about moving. Not just moving house again but moving away. She'd heard that Pop was seeing a girlfriend of hers, and suddenly it seemed there were ghosts and old boyfriends around every corner. New York was finished for her.

Two weeks later, Catherine came into our room in the middle of the night. She turned my bedside table light on and sat down next to me. She was crying.

"I just want you to know that your momma fired me and I love you both."

I was still half-asleep as she gathered me up in her tree-like arms and crushed me against her immense bosom. I reached my arms around her neck and held her. I remembered all the times she'd made us that special syrup when we were sick, cooked our breakfast, and helped us find our shoes. She tucked me back into bed and kissed the top of my head. Then she gave my sister the same farewell. She turned out the light and waddled to the door.

"Bless you, my lambie pies," she said in the dark.

Catherine was leaving us, and we would never see her again. Feeling such sorrow that she wouldn't be in the kitchen in the morning, or anyplace else in our lives, my heart felt pressed down upon, as if the heaviest book in the world had been placed there. Utterly bereft, my sister and I cried quietly into our pillows.

The next day, when Robbie and I came home from school, I spied a large pile of familiar-looking Louis Vuitton luggage heaped in a corner of the lobby as we walked through to the elevator. I glanced over at Johnny the doorman, wondering if he might want to tell me something, but he just clasped his arms behind his back and looked out through the door at the street. When we got upstairs, we discovered our front door open and the apartment completely empty.

"Is this our house?" my sister said. She took her coat off and, seeing nowhere to put it, plopped it down on the floor.

"I think so," I said, looking around.

We were standing in the foyer wondering if we'd been robbed when Mother emerged from her bedroom with her mink coat over her arm.

"Oh, there you are," she said, checking her watch.

"Where is . . . everything?" I asked. All that was left were the nails in the walls where the pictures had once hung, and little dust balls on the floor that had previously been trapped by pieces of furniture. Even the piano was gone. It made me think of what the Grinch did to Whoville.

"The movers came today and I had it all put into storage."

The elevator man walked by with another suitcase and our cat, Maudie, in her carrier, yowling like an angry baby. Maudie was a chocolate-point Siamese and always meowed loudly like a person who wouldn't be ignored. I ran to my room to see if anything had been left behind, but it was empty.

"Wendy? Where are you?" I heard my mother's shoes clicking down the hallway toward me. I looked up to the top of the bookshelf where our stash of secret saved toys was hidden. They would have to stay behind now. Mother came into the empty room, her voice echoing off the bare walls: "You see, all gone. Now hurry because I have a taxi waiting downstairs."

"Yes, ma'am." I followed her down the hall and out the front door of the apartment. I imagined another little girl, the next little girl, finding the angel dolls and the teddy bear, like a hidden treasure.

We all got into the elevator and went downstairs, where we said good-bye to Johnny the doorman, who held open the door of the taxi that was to take us to our new home: the Croyden Hotel on East Eighty-sixth Street and Fifth Avenue.

"You'll love it there," said Mother as we barreled down Park Avenue. "There's a gift shop in the lobby, and there's a movie theater right around the corner."

My sister and I stared dumbly at her. This morning we'd left our home to go to school, and at the end of the day we had a new one. Maudie was wailing from her carrier on the front seat next to the driver. I understood exactly how she felt.

As promised, a gift shop was in the lobby—more of a newsstand really—where Robbie and I lingered while Mother checked in. Our eyes roved over the *Tiger Beats*, *True Romance* comics, Chiclets and Chunkys, as the reality of our collective fate sunk in.

"We can get room service," I told Robbie, reverting to my Little Mary Sunshine routine as I always did at moments of massive upheaval.

"Like Eloise," Robbie said glumly.

"And the maid will clean up our room," I chirped.

I pointed out to her that this meant no more being chased around by Catherine telling us our room was a pigsty and trying to smack our bottoms with a tea towel as we screamed and ran away. I was trying to melt Robbie's sadness through sheer perkiness and it worked.

She looked at me and her mouth popped open. "We can make as many spitballs as we want."

Catherine used to get furious when we threw wet wads of toilet paper up onto the ceiling. The balls either fell to the floor, making a ploppy mess, or fused to the ceiling, making them impossible to remove.

Now, breakfast was an Entenmann's chocolate doughnut and a glass of Tropicana orange juice from the little fridge in our kitchenette. All our other meals were ordered over the phone from the restaurant in the lobby, and the hotel did our laundry.

Four weeks later, on our last day of school, we came home and couldn't find Maudie. She usually ran to the door to greet us, meowing hello and rubbing against our kneesocks. We looked under the bed, in the closets, and even in the hallway outside the door. We were about to call the front desk to report her missing when Mother came home. Robbie and I ran up to her and told her we couldn't find Maudie.

"I had to give her away," Mother said. She stood by the hall table, dressed in a khaki-colored Yves Saint Laurent linen trouser suit with her Vuitton purse hanging in the crook of her arm, and started to remove her thin leather gloves, pulling at them one finger at a time. "But don't worry, she'll be fine. I gave her to Joy Wallace, remember her? She has three girls so Maudie will have lots of playmates."

"But why did you give her away?" Joy Wallace's bratty kids weren't deserving playmates for our Maudie. The youngest one, Caroline, had pulled her pants down and bent over to show her tushie at the dinner table the last time we were over at their house.

Mother explained that we couldn't take Maudie with us because of a quarantine on animals coming from America. I didn't know what she was talking about. From her purse she produced three pieces of paper. She placed them down on the table with a snap, raised her eyebrows, and glanced down at us as if she had produced the winning hand in a high-stakes card game. I looked at them. They were tickets to sail on the *Queen Elizabeth 2*—boarding in two days. "We're moving to England. London, to be exact." Mother thrust her gloves into her handbag and walked down the long hallway to her bedroom. Robbie and I followed her.

"What about the summer with Daddy?" I asked.

She started taking off her jewelry as she kicked off her shoes. "Well, you're not going this summer. Your father's getting remarried and he's too busy to take care of you."

"Did he say that?" I asked, suddenly worried and trying to puzzle it out.

"How come he doesn't want to see us?" Robbie asked.

"He has a new family now, I guess. New wife, a new son, and two daughters, from what I hear." Mother shrugged her shoulders as if it were just too bad. Robbie and I stood watching her get undressed. She put on a peach-colored silk robe and went into her bathroom. I heard the faucets turn on and water running into the tub. I felt as if we were on a speeding train that was going so fast we couldn't see the scenery hurtling by—it was just a blur and any second we would jump the rails. A hundred questions raced through my mind and yet I couldn't think of what to say.

The water stopped running and Mother reentered the room. She lit a cigarette and paced up and down on the white carpet for a moment, regarding us forlornly.

"I can see that you're both upset." She stamped the cigarette out in the hotel ashtray by her bed. "I can't think of any other way to tell you this."

"Tell us what?" For a second I thought that maybe Daddy was dead.

Then she opened her arms and gathered us to her. She

sighed, hugging us tight. "I know it's hard," she whispered. "But you girls are just going to have to accept the fact that your father doesn't really care about you." She loosened her grip and looked in our eyes.

"That's not true," Robbie said, chin trembling.

I looked at her, surprised, not sure if this was defiance or disbelief. She may have felt, like me, as if it all couldn't be happening. But unlike me, she had voiced it.

Mother, her mind halfway across the Atlantic already, took it in stride. "I'm afraid it is true, and I love you both too much to lie to you anymore." She shook her head slowly while she said this to us, as if she had to tell us that the cookie jar was empty and there wasn't anything left for us. "One day, when you're older, you'll see that I'm doing what's best. We'll go far away where he can't hurt us anymore."

"But we don't want to go far away," I said.

"How far away?" Robbie asked. "Can we call him on the telephone and say good-bye?"

"Yes, I want to say good-bye to Daddy, too," I pleaded.

Mother's shoulders drooped slightly and she looked back and forth between me and Robbie, clearly weighing something in her mind. She sighed deeply, then said, "I had hoped to wait until you were older, but maybe it's best this way."

She went to her vanity table, removed her wallet from her purse, and unzipped it. She pulled out a black-and-white photograph of herself with a strange man. We stared at the picture in her hand. The man was slim and darkly handsome, dressed in a suit. His hair was slicked back like a crooner's. I could tell from Mother's dress and hairdo that the picture had been taken some time ago. In the photo, they were looking at each other with one arm around each other's waist like they were the only two people in the world.

"Who is that?" Robbie's brow furrowed as she peered at the snapshot.

Mother looked hard at my sister and said to her, "That's your father, your real father." We both looked at the picture for another moment, then Mother put it back in her wallet. She told us his name was Nick and he was an old boyfriend of hers. He was Greek. "Your father was gone so much and I was lonely. I warned him that something might happen. But he didn't care." She said this as if it were all Daddy's fault. My sister started to whimper and my mother smiled at her and knelt in front of her, shushing her. "You know," Mother said, stroking my sister's hair, "you shouldn't be sad, because you were truly a child of love."

These were her words of comfort to my sister, and then, as if to soften the blow even further, she added, "And Wendy wasn't." This information didn't reassure Robbie and she fled from the room, sobbing. Stinging from the cruelty of Mother's remark, my cheeks reddened with humiliation. I stood rooted to the carpet, unable to move, like a character in a cartoon who can't run away from the monster.

"If he really loved you girls, he never would have let me go." With that, Mother went to take her bath.

I tried to breathe, but I couldn't. I felt that all the air had been punched out of me. I was outside of my body, float-ing, pressed up against the ceiling and looking down at my-self—trapped between the faint sounds of my sister crying her ten-year-old heart out and my mother splashing in the bath. I don't know how long it lasted, but I felt I was filling up with something, an idea, a realization that Robbie and I were completely on our own.

I turned and ran. When I got to our room, I found Robbie weeping on the bed. I went over to my sister and put my arms around her and told her it wasn't true—we were real sisters and it wasn't true. I was lying; I knew it was true. She looked just like the smiling man in the photo.

LONDON, 1971

chapter five

AMERICAN DIVORCÉE
IN LONDON

The wind whipped our hair and stung our faces as we stood on the gleaming deck of the *Queen Elizabeth 2*, sailing out of New York harbor. A welcoming face to so many, the Statue of Liberty with her spearlike crown and stern expression looked, to Robbie and me, as though she might whack us with her big torch or step on us with her giant sandal.

Our excitement at the novelty of being on an ocean liner was tempered by a melancholy we both felt over all the people and places we were leaving behind. I hadn't gotten to say good-bye to my best friend, Linda Miller, and her two miniature collies we used to take for walks around her block. Robbie had wanted to visit the merry-go-round in Central Park one last time and had forgotten to bid farewell to Morey, the old gentleman who gave us free candy at the newsstand in our old lobby. Most of all, Robbie and I missed

Daddy and ached for the summer we would not have with him. In the taxi on our way to the boat, in an effort to beat back our building emotions and trembling lips, Mother had reiterated the hard facts: our father didn't care about us, and we had been replaced by his new family. We did not want to believe it, but had no evidence to the contrary. No letter, no phone call, no bon voyage.

And so the specter of our father traveled with us, like a ghost whose presence you sense, but never see.

Since the awful revelation of Robbie's mystery father, we had tacitly agreed that it was never to be spoken of. I had assured her that it wasn't true and told her that I didn't believe it. The most important thing was that we were sisters, a team, and we needed to stick together.

To steel ourselves against the sadness we felt about leaving, we turned the voyage into a game. The *QE2* was like a small, shiny city, and we capered all over her looking for fun and adventure. We stuffed notes into bottles and tossed them overboard, wondering if they would float all the way to China. We pretended to be spies and eavesdropped on other passengers lounging in their deck chairs or drinking in the cocktail lounge. We went to see *Fiddler on the Roof* in the ship cinema so many times, we could act out all the songs complete with choreography in our stateroom, jumping back and forth on the twin beds, singing, before collapsing in heaps of breathless laughter.

We were traveling in first class ("Thank God," Mother pointed out more than once). We dined in the grand

Britannica Room, which had floor-to-ceiling windows that looked out onto the Atlantic, and were waited on by young black men in starched coats and white gloves, the white bright against their dark skin.

On the last night of our voyage there was a fancy buffet dinner for the guests. It was a smorgasbord of golden roast ducks and turkeys, whole suckling pigs with apples in their mouths, and rows of long, poached salmons with cucumber scales and green cocktail olives for eyes. Pink lobsters lay on rafts of jiggly aspic, and mounds of shrimp all stared blankly through black bead eyes. Each cooked beast was manned by a server wearing a puffy chef hat and wielding a carving knife that he sharpened dramatically in the air, making it look like the beginning of some strange sword dance or offering ceremony to the gods of the sea. Vegetables steamed in silver chafing dishes—asparagus as thin as soda straws, haricots verts glistening with butter and spotted with slivered almonds, and crusty broiled tomatoes served alongside four different kinds of potatoes. I had never seen so much food in one place. A separate table was just for the desserts. In the center, surrounded by mounds of profiteroles, Bavarian creams, and babas au rhum, stood a two-foot-tall, all-white cake in the shape of a swan.

My sister and I gasped, being careful not to point—a punishable offense. If we were to be less than perfect and behave rudely, it would reflect poorly upon Mother and there would be a price to pay—maybe not here, in the fancy dining room in front of other first-class travelers, but when we returned to our stateroom.

Since our parents' divorce, Mother had occasionally spanked us with a hairbrush, which, according to the way she had been raised, was a mild form of punishment. She had also sent us to bed without supper. But refusing to speak to us for extended periods was her most effective tactic. It made us feel small, almost like we'd disappeared. The threat of being abandoned by the only parent left in our lives was far more frightening than anything else. It was this fear that kept us in check.

All during dinner we stared at the cake, which looked as if it had just flown in from the land of the Sugar Plum Fairy. After we had eaten, we excused ourselves from the table and held hands as we walked over to gaze upon its sweet loveliness. The swan was gliding across a lake of spun sugar, its iced wings raised as if it had just landed there. Its wings were adorned with baby pink roses made of sugar. Robin and I stood in front of it mesmerized and asked the young man behind the table if we could have some.

He laughed at us, his white teeth smiling. "Oh, you don't want to eat that, misses." His West Indian accent reminded me of our nanny Catherine's.

"Pleeeease," we begged, holding plates from the buffet table up to him for our pieces of cake.

"No, you don't want that." He waved us away with his gloved hand. "It's just for show. It is not . . . real."

We looked at him confused. It sure looked like cake.

"What's it made out of?" Robin asked, flashing her most

innocent smile. I followed suit, hoping we could kill him with cuteness.

"Chicken fat, miss." Our smiles vanished. "I'm afraid it's only to look at, miss."

Disappointed, we took some chocolate mousse and returned to our table, where Mother was in mid-dazzle, explaining to a handsome man in an expensive suit that we'd all grown tired of dreary New York and were moving to London for a change of pace. "Isn't that right, darlings?" she said, turning to us, her well-turned-out daughters. We nodded and smiled as required, a smear of chocolate mousse on Robbie's upper lip the only piece of the picture out of place. The handsome man grinned at us and returned his gaze to Mother. She worked her smoke-and-mirrors magic, presenting a sleek image to the world, but the truth was that we were just as fake as that swan.

At night before bed, my sister and I would watch the dolphins, shiny in the moonlight, swimming alongside the ship outside our porthole. Unlike us, they seemed to know where they were going.

Our first flat in London was a posh town house on Cadogan Place, near Sloane Square—the future stomping ground of Princess Diana and the other Sloane Rangers. It was a short taxi ride from Harrods or, if Mother was interested in some hip slumming, the King's Road. Glitter rock was all over the radio, and *Monty Python* had just started playing on the BBC.

Once ensconced, Mother immersed herself in the glam life. In the same way she had reinvented herself in New York as a trophy wife and divorcée, in London she stepped into the role of the madcap American with two ex-husbands. She was thirty-three, looked twenty-five, and had a small fortune to spend—compensation, of course, for her suffering.

We'd see Mother fleetingly at breakfast and then again when she'd blow a kiss good-bye to us over our supper plates on her way out the door. Out front, a big black cab or a hired Bentley, depending on her destination, waited to take her to another marvelous party.

While she was gone, we were left with Serena, a smoky Irish stunner Mother had found at an agency. She was gorgeous, with long black hair, Barbra Streisand fingernails, and green eyes. As soon as Mother would leave, Serena would ring her boyfriend, and he would come 'round with the fancy Rolls-Royce that he drove for a living. His name was Fergus. He would sit on the sofa in his black uniform with his cap perched on his knee and drink whiskey from a flask and smoke. Serena would sit on his lap filing her claws, and he'd tell us funny stories about something called the Irish Republican Army. Fergus told us it was an independence movement that was fighting to free the Irish from British rule. He had quite a few friends and family members in the IRA and explained to us what they did to the people who betrayed them. From Fergus we learned how to recognize people who'd been kneecapped (they limped), what happened to men on a hunger strike in prison (they had tubes shoved down their throats), and, by the way, did we know how horses were gelded?

Over breakfast one morning, Mother discovered all the interesting facts we were learning from Fergus while in the company of Serena, and she was, of course, let go. It wasn't the breaking of knees or the gruesome prison force-feeding stories that concerned her, it was all the talk of Ireland. Mother blamed the whole country of Ireland for her two marriages to men of Irish descent not having worked out. "Never marry an Irishman" and "Never marry an actor" were oft-repeated bits of advice, punctuated for emphasis by a jab of the tortoiseshell-and-gold cigarette holder she'd taken to using.

Our days of babysitters finally came to a halt when we told Mother that Serena's replacement, Alice—we called her Ashtray Alice—liked to put on fashion shows with us.

"How nice," said Mother, envisioning the good clean fun we were having with Alice, who was an elderly lady with white hair and glasses on a chain around her neck.

Then we told her that during the fashion show Alice took off her top and paraded up and down the room in her bra on an imaginary runway, describing her outfit while using a heavy glass ashtray as her microphone. She always held the ashtray right up to her lips, which made her voice sound all breathy. Then Robbie and I would do the same—walk up and down the runway with our tops off as Alice continued the fashion commentary with her ashtray.

"How disgusting," said Mother. Instead of hiring a

granny to watch us, Mother had engaged a kinky lesbian. No more babysitters after that; we were to be latchkey kids. Mother reasoned that London was a much safer city than New York anyway and that we were old enough to take care of ourselves.

Being the seasoned city kids we were, Robbie and I came up with our own safety techniques. When we were out and about, saying "Wooden button" was code for when someone potentially creepy or perverted was following us. That was the signal to change trains, cross the street, or go in the opposite direction. "Hippie hair spray" meant we smelled a person wearing patchouli, which we perceived as something drug addicts wore to identify themselves to each other. Whispering "Eighty-six" meant it was time to go. Of course, sometimes there were no words, like when, at the bottom of the long, clacking escalator in the South Kensington tube station, a man flashed us. He opened his raincoat. We looked. He smiled. We screamed and ran for the train to school.

While Mother was partying and simultaneously dating a dashing Romanian polo player and a fey English solicitor who wore an ascot and a monocle, Robin and I attended the American School in London, in St. John's Wood, with the children of oil executives, diplomats, and even a few movie stars.

Our first day of school, it was clear we were encountering a new breed of rich kid. We showed up to find that although we thought of ourselves as cosmopolitan New Yorkers, we weren't nearly as worldly as these kids were. Like us, they'd had moved around a lot, but to places like Germany, Libya, Japan, and Nairobi. And unlike our old school, Town, ASL was enormous, with a student body of over a thousand. And every single one of them seemed cooler than we were. We needed a way in.

In an astounding moment of sheer luck, our mother bumped into Judy Turner—a former beauty queen and wife of a Texas oil executive—shopping at Harvey Nichols, the upscale department store rival to Harrods. They immediately bonded over their American accents, big hair, and penchant for Sonia Rykiel knitwear. The day after this meeting, which had resulted in a shopping spree that almost reduced Mother's charge card to ashes and was followed by a ladies' heart-to-heart in a Knightsbridge wine bar, Judy's daughter, Tracy, walked up to Robbie and me in the cafeteria at school and did what she had been instructed to do.

"Hi," she drawled, as we looked up at her over our plates of chicken curry and chips.

Tracy Turner was the most glamorous and beautiful girl our age. She was thin and willowy, with long, caramel-colored hair, tanned skin, perfect teeth, and a nose that turned just ever so slightly up at the end. She was like the girl from Ipanema—whenever she walked by, everyone would go "Ah."

I glanced around to make sure she wasn't talking to someone else. "Hi," I blurted back, regaining my composure.

"Are you those new girls, Wendy and Robin from New

York?" Everyone stopped and stared because the It girl was speaking to us. Robbie practically spit-taked her Fanta.

"Um, yes, we are," I answered haltingly. I noticed that she kind of shone, as if she were on the red carpet under a follow spot or something.

"Well, I was wondering if you wanted to come over to my house this afternoon. I have some new records we could listen to while we do our homework." She put one hand on her hip and used the other to adjust her leather-fringed handbag.

"Wow, we'd love to. Thanks." Robbie and I smiled and nodded.

"Great. See you after school." She flounced off, executing a perfect hair toss on her way out of the lunchroom.

And that was it. We were in.

Tracy welcomed us into her large posse of girlfriends, which included the wildly popular Cassidy girls, Lynn and Diane, whose international banker dad hunted big game in Africa in his spare time; Lourdes Lopez, a red-haired Mexican spitfire; and Paige Dundee, whose parents were rumored to be spies for the CIA. Our moms all became friends, and many of our weekends were full of sleepovers, shopping at Selfridges or Way In, or just hanging out at Lynn and Diane's listening to music and watching them feed live mice to their pet boa constrictor. There always seemed to be exciting people there, like the dishy actor John Phillip Law from the *Sinbad* films, or tall, toothy Jeremy Lloyd, a writer and actor who had been in *A Hard Day's Night* with the Beatles. Robbie and I begged Mother for a whole new wardrobe just to keep up.

The other thing besides size that made ASL different from our school in New York was bling: music and art classes, sports teams, a state-of-the-art gymnasium, a theater with a thrust stage, and tons of money for field trips.

In my English class, we were reading *Macbeth*, so our teacher, Mr. Jesse, took us to see the play at the Royal Shakespeare Company, with Nicol Williamson and Helen Mirren starring. It was my first exposure to Shakespeare since watching my dad onstage at the Guthrie. This made me instantly adore Mr. Jesse, who was unlike any other teacher I had ever had. He was in his forties, short and compact, always clad in jeans and turtlenecks. He changed the way he looked every few weeks by growing a beard, shaving his head, or sporting a Fu Manchu mustache or a goatee. Always in motion, he feverishly spouted poetry like a crazed beat poet, pacing inside the circle our desks made.

"'My name is Ozymandias, king of kings: Look upon my works, ye Mighty, and despair!'" Mr. Jesse boomed.

He'd throw the dictionary at you if you didn't know a word, shouting, "Look it up!" He told us he divorced his wife because she used too many three-letter words.

One day after class he called me over. "This story you wrote, Wendy, is really very good." He handed the pages back to me.

"Thank you, Mr. Jesse," I said shyly.

"I showed it to a friend of mine, an actor, who thought it was wonderful. You should keep writing, my dear."

"Yes, sir." It meant the world to me that he liked my story.

"Life is short, and one musn't squander one's talents, don't you agree?" He arched his eyebrows and scratched the muttonchop sideburns that he had recently grown.

"No, sir, I won't." I was too afraid to tell him I didn't know what *squander* meant.

I continued to struggle in math and flunked algebra. Twice. Math made me cry, but I adored history, French, and Mr. Jesse.

My sister's attitude toward school was similar to the one she had toward her appearance—she didn't care. Or at least she didn't care about what other people—her teachers and Mother—thought she should care about. Where my years of being a goody-goody made me the perfect student capable of delivering exactly what was asked for, Robbie had evolved into a more out-of-the-box thinker, preferring her own ideas to those of others. I kind of admired her for it, but was also afraid. We were teenagers now, and Robbie was stepping out more. I couldn't shield her from poor grades or from Mother's reaction to them. Report cards were the one thing Mother noticed during this time, and they sparked a long-simmering battle between her and my sister.

"Are you telling me that this is the best you can do?" Mother shook Robbie's B's and C's report card at her angrily.

"Yes, Mother!" she said tearily.

"Do you know what would have happened to me if I had brought home a report card like this? I was a straight-A student!"

"I'm sorry, I'll try harder next time." Robbie ran to her room, crying, and closed the door.

"I'll help her study, Mother," I pleaded on my sister's behalf. Mother stalked off in a huff, late for her ladies' brunch, slamming the door behind her.

These occasional outbursts over my sister's grades at school and others about the tidiness of our bedrooms were short-lived and for the first time we were able to let our guard down a bit. Compared with the past, these were honeymoon years for Robbie and me. The usual tension and fear of Mother's disapproval began to ease, as Mother became even less interested in her role as a mother and reworked herself as a jet-setter.

Mother's best friend and main guide through swinging London was Mary Broomfield, who was an upscale concierge at the London Hilton, helping the crème de la crème solve their high-class problems. Mary had found us our first strategically placed, trendy flat in London. She was a statuesque Brit with a helmet hairdo who looked a bit like Agnes Moorehead but with larger teeth. Mary came from an upper-class family, but had been forced to go to work when the family money ran out and her husband went down in an RAF plane. She was very well connected and introduced Mother to an international cast of characters who joined her entourage of other groovy American expat moms.

Deziah was a psychic to the royals who wore her hennaed hair and Gypsy dresses long. Mother started telephoning her every morning to see if she should venture out to this or that event. "Deziah says there'll be bad vibes there," Mother would say, putting down the receiver. Fresh-faced brunette Hilary Mole looked like a kindergarten teacher but had been a high-priced call girl who was now safely married to a famous bandleader who had once been one of her clients. Dominique Lamond was a volatile French department-store heiress who looked like Anouk Aimée and swore and drank like a sailor, and whom I frequently found passed out in the downstairs loo.

Mother also became fast friends with Marian Montgomery, the American singer, and started going to Ronnie Scott's jazz club in Soho to see her perform, with her girlfriends in tow. From there, they'd move on to exclusive discos like Annabel's or Tramp and often end the evening at our house to drink the rest of the night away. On Sundays, they would all come to what Mother began calling the "drunken lunch" in our garden with cold white wine, cigarettes, and maybe a chicken salad for those who were hungry.

Left to our own devices, my sister and I emulated the values and behavior of the only role model we had; Mother was out on her party circuit, so we created our own. It was easy to meet up at someone's parent-free house and break into the liquor cabinet. I liked Mateus rosé because it was sweet and came in a curvy bottle, but sometimes we'd just pour a bit of everything in a tall glass and take turns sipping. The first time I was actually served alcohol—Dom Pérignon at a brunch at Mary Broomfield's house—I felt so sick from drinking the night before, I poured it into a plant when no one was looking.

Robbie and I also attempted to copy Mother's clothes-horse side. She was sporting Ossie Clark, Yves Saint Laurent, and Courrèges, so we started shopping at a kids' clothing boutique named, appropriately enough, Little Horrors, the Kitson of its time. We bought trendy French New Man corduroy pants with matching jackets, and flowered Cacharel blouses to wear to school. For my first big formal party, thrown by the son of a diplomat at Quaglino's, an exclusive Soho supper club, I went to Biba to buy a long dress and a beaded evening bag. Biba was simply one of the most fashionable shops in London. Twiggy had appeared in their ad campaign and their logo was of a glamorous couple dancing who were dressed like Fred and Ginger.

And, of course, we smoked. We especially liked these herbal cigarettes that came in a flowered box and smelled like overcooked vegetables. Who cared if they tasted like burnt broccoli; we thought we looked so cool smoking. At the pub, conveniently located inside the tube station across the road from school, we were always trying to find someone to buy us a shandy, beer mixed with ginger beer, or a Babycham, which was sparkling pear juice with a cute fawn on the bottle. We had even purchased platform shoes, hoping to look older (taller) and sometimes it worked. I realize now we probably looked a lot like Jodi Foster in *Taxi Driver.*

Another favorite pastime was chasing pop stars. When Elton John gave a concert in the ASL gym, Robbie and

I ran outside at the end of the show to the back entrance, determined to get his autograph. "I love you, Elton!" I yelled, jumping in front of him as he came flying out of the exit. Startled, he tripped over me in his silver platform boots and matching pants. I can still see his shiny bottom flying away from me. I didn't get his autograph, but our eyes met as he looked at me over his shoulder while he was dragged off by bodyguards. For weeks, I held out hope that he would come find me like the prince in *Cinderella* searching for his one true love.

I always went for the pansexual guys who wore makeup, big shoes, and glitter: Elton, Roxy Music, T. Rex, and David Bowie. Even at fourteen, I knew you couldn't help whom you fell in love with. My friend Lynn Cassidy was hopelessly gaga over Donny Osmond, who I thought was too perfect with his straight teeth and bowl haircut. At night, before she went to bed, she listened to him croon "Sweet and Innocent" on her stereo and then kissed the thirty-five Donny posters on her walls good night. When we discovered the Osmonds were coming to London, we mobilized at the Cassidys' house to make a plan.

"How are we going to meet them?" screeched Lynn. We plowed through many bags of crisps and bottles of soda trying to strategize. It was important that we not have a repeat of our botched attempt to meet the Jackson Five at Heathrow a few months before. Having gotten up at 4:00 a.m., we were only able to get close enough to see five Afro'ed heads cross the tarmac. I was devastated.

"Let's just go over there. Maybe we'll think of something on the way," said Lynn's little sister, Diane, sweetly. We all jumped on the tube, heading for the Churchill Hotel. When we got there, it was completely surrounded by hundreds of screaming, crying girls. Bobbies were trying to keep the "weenyboppers" (as Donny's followers had been dubbed in the British press) back, and television crews were filming. It was a circus.

"Look, they're letting taxis through," said Robbie, characteristically observant. It was often my sister's diabolical genius that set the plans in motion. "What if we pretended to be hotel guests, getting out of a cab?"

"Outstanding!" cried Lynn.

We ran down the block, tearing past the hotel and the screaming mob, and hailed a taxi. We gave the driver five pounds to drive us up to the entrance of the hotel. Less than a minute later, the top-hatted doorman at the Churchill was opening the taxi door and welcoming us. We headed through the lobby, straight to the elevator, having no idea what floor they were on.

"Let's start at the top," Lynn said, punching the highest floor. When we got out, it was too quiet, so we started running down the stairs, stopping to check every floor for Osmonds. Five flights down, security men were sitting on folding chairs in the hall. We thought we were busted, but they were so impressed that we had made it this far that they let us stay for a while and hang out. Jimmy, Donny's little brother, was playing basketball in the hall. Robin stuck her head out the window, and the girls below went wild thinking she was an Osmond.

"You girls want to meet Donny?" The rest of us didn't care, but Lynn did, so she went to meet her dream man. Afterward, she was all flushed and gooey-eyed. We rode down in the elevator in silence, Lynn, on cloud nine, ecstatically dreaming of being Mrs. Donny Osmond, and Robin and I thinking of how much fun it had been breaking and entering.

chapter six

CHANEL BONFIRE

When Mother became restless or bored, or if she was avoiding a lover or was too afraid to open her American Express bill, we'd skip town. Most often, we'd go to Paris. Like the spoiled American teenagers we were, Robbie and I soon began to whine about having to go: "The waiters are so rude! The toilet paper's waxy! What about Italy? Or Spain?!" Finally, at one point we refused to go.

"Leave us here; it's only two days," we said before one early-fall weekend. There was going to be a big party that weekend with hot boys we did not want to miss. We had even bought new hip-huggers to wear.

"It may not be two days this time. I have to go on business," Mother replied.

Business? I thought. *Like working? For money?* Mother had once sold a few poems when we were small, but *busi-*

ness was not a word anyone would associate with anything Mother did.

"Pack for a week. We leave in an hour," she said.

The next morning we were checked into the Hôtel Sydney Opéra, a stuffy little box of a hotel, not at all Mother's usual style, and she was leaving us for her "business" meeting, which, it turned out, was at the Hôtel Ritz bar. I wondered about her choice of a clingy, fuchsia, Pucci print dress and an excessive amount of Chanel No. 19, but said nothing.

Paris was having a heat wave and the Hôtel Sydney Opéra wasn't air-conditioned, so Robbie and I lay around our room in our underwear. Unlike me, and much to my dismay, Robbie had started wearing a bra, having recently developed boobs. I was a little jealous.

We dug into some cold roast chicken and chunks of Doux de Montagne from the restaurant downstairs.

"Wait a minute," she said, "why don't we pretend that we're Henry VIII and eat with our hands like they did back then?" Robbie was learning about the Tudors in her history class.

"Yeah!" It sounded like fun. We stretched out on the bed, semi-naked, and chewed on chicken bones and bread, pretending to be English royalty. But what to do with the bones? Robbie informed me that in the great dining hall of Hampton Court, Henry simply tossed the bones over his shoulder onto the floor.

"Really?"

"Yeah, like this." Robin expertly flung her chicken bone over her shoulder out the open window.

"Well done!" We both laughed and rolled on the bed, nibbling at the bones and then throwing them out the window with Tudoresque flourish.

My sister's fast track to puberty, and her rebellious nature, seemed to diminish the difference in our ages. While we had left New York very much the older and younger sisters, we were now becoming more of a unit—the dynamic duo, laughing and tossing our bones at the world.

We were just finishing the last of the cheese, giggling and licking our fingers, when loud stomping and angry French voices came down the hall, followed by pounding on our door.

"*Ouvrez cette porte tout de suite, mesdemoiselles!*"

Thinking that a mob with torches and pitchforks was about to break in and see us naked—a fate worse than death—we screamed and threw on our clothes.

A look through the peephole revealed the mob to be the concierge, manager, and room-service waiter. Despite that our school French hadn't included so much cursing, we were able to decipher that our window opened onto the air shaft where the hotel dried its clean linen. We ran to the window and looked down to see white sheets stained with grease and strewn with chicken bones. Mortified and a little terrified, we slumped to the floor with our backs against the door, afraid to open it.

The shouting continued until I heard a familiar voice arguing in French with the hotel staff. As the staff's anger was checked and their grumbling voices moved away, the voice switched to English. "Jesus, Georgann, this place is a shit-hole! You're damn lucky I'm here."

We opened the door to find Pop, our now ex-stepfather, standing there with Mother's suitcase. "Hello, dearies, we're getting you out of here," he said happily, playing the knight in shining armor ready to whisk us all away from the dangers of a second-class hotel.

We had heard that, after a brief shot at reconciling with his first wife, Pop had married that old girlfriend of Mother's and they had had a child, so we were a little mystified by his arm around mother's waist after a five-year hiatus. Being relatively young, and at times on the wrong side of her angry rages, I couldn't fully appreciate Mother's appeal to men or her ability to wield it. She may not have been much of a businessperson in the usual sense, but clearly she had struck quite a deal at the bar at the Ritz. So a half hour later, Robbie and I were in a spacious, sunlit room at the InterContinental, looking out at the Tuileries from our balcony window, and drinking Coca-Colas we'd ordered from room service.

Pop took us to Cartier on the swanky rue de la Paix and bought both of us gold charm bracelets with little French flags on them. He also bought Mother a grape-size sapphire ring that was surrounded by diamonds.

The next morning, we were eating croissants slathered in jam and trashy American cereal at the rolling table from room service when the door flew open and Mother entered dramatically. She was wearing a luxurious hotel terry-cloth robe, her makeup slightly smudged, her hair pillow-rumpled.

"Girls?" She seemed to be in speech mode.

We sipped our orange juice and waited for her to begin.

"Are you happy to see Pop?"

It was a silly question. Although he had been in our lives briefly, we loved Pop because he was the only stepfather we knew. He laughed at all our jokes and was fun to be around, and he bought us stuff. So we nodded and continued eating.

"He still loves me and can't live without me." Mother paced and smiled, tugging at her cigarette. "So, we're going to try to work it out." She turned to us and opened her arms, looking wildly happy. On cue, my sister and I got up from the breakfast table and ran to her embrace. We were a little confused, but if she was happy, what the hell, we went with it.

So after a five-year absence from our lives, Pop had rematerialized as our fairy ex-stepfather. Suddenly it became not unusual for us to come home from school to find Pop sitting in our living room in London, with a lit Gitanes and a Tanqueray martini nearby. After he'd left, Mother would say, "You know he loves you two so much."

"We know, Mother," we dutifully replied. I was pretty sure that it wasn't just Pop's love for me and Robin that kept him hanging around. There had to be another reason he continued to pay for our private school and summer camp in Switzerland. Even if Mother was seeing several men simultaneously, and she always was, she managed to keep Pop on the back burner—just in case she needed him.

It was quite a juggling act. They seemed to fight as much as they didn't but always ended up in each other's arms. It seemed they couldn't be together and they couldn't be apart. And so they entered a phase of being together some of the time, and then apart some of the time. Pop would go away—and then he would come back. The Atlantic Ocean seemed to make the relationship possible. Where others might see an unfathomable obstacle, they found convenience. I think she loved him for changing her life and showing her the world outside of her small town in the Midwest; but I couldn't be sure. There was a strong connection between them that was beyond my girlish understanding. Maybe he was the only person who understood her. I would never know.

"I think he loves you as if you were his own children," she said to us one day after he'd left. As if to further this feeling, Mother sent a letter to our school and had our last names changed to his, Rea. She talked about his formally adopting us, which never happened, and I didn't know if it was even true or something she'd made up. I strongly suspected this idea had a financial aspect: we would legally be tied to him, even though she no longer was. And as she was always in survival mode, that would be a boon to her.

We didn't have a father in our lives, so it was fun to have Pop, though he was more like a stand-in for the real thing. Like a jolly uncle or an old family friend, he was the guy who would show up to take you to the circus, or out to your favorite restaurant on your birthday. Our image of our own father was starting to fade away. We had no photos of him, and trying to conjure his face in our minds was becoming more and more difficult. Pop seemed to enjoy his paternal role with us when he was around, and we had to take what we could get.

Like all fairy tales in which Mother was a player, this latest with Pop would be brief and cautionary. At our next spring break, he appeared with tickets to Morocco. He said he was scouting for land there to build a resort and we could come along for the ride. The plane stopped in Gibraltar to refuel, and Pop took us out on the tarmac to see the Barbary apes. We stood on the airport's only runway, surrounded by the ocean on three sides. Pop pointed at the Rock of Gibraltar, and at first Robin and I couldn't see them. Then little brown dots appeared to be scuttling all over the giant rock in a kind of figure-eight pattern, continuously swooping over the rock the way birds do in the air. We were amazed, having only seen wild animals in the zoo. Pop seemed happy to have shown us something new. He put his arms around us, sharing our delighted wonder.

We reboarded and a few hours later arrived in the Moroccan coastal town of Agadir, on the Atlantic Ocean, where we spent a week at Club Med, which at that time was considered more cosmopolitan and exclusive than it is now. In the morning Pop would hand us ropes of plastic pop-it beads, which was the currency of the club, so we could buy lunch, drinks, trapeze lessons—whatever we wanted. Then he and Mother went off in a car Pop had rented that was the size of a washing machine, searching for the perfect piece of land.

Our first day, Robbie and I met some cute American boys a little older than we were who started talking to us in the pool. Their names were Nat and Tommy Ellenoff. They were tall and skinny and lived in New York.

"So where are you guys from?" asked Nat. He was the older one. I never knew how to answer this question. Which of the four cities we had already lived in was the one we were from? I decided to keep it simple.

"Well, we're actually from New York, too." We all got out of the pool.

"Wow, that's weird. Where do you go to school?" Tommy was rubbing his chest with a towel. Water dripped from the ends of his curly, dark hair.

"Town," I said.

"But actually we live in London now," added Robin as she fidgeted with her bikini bottom. I flipped my wet hair behind my shoulder and twisted the water out of it.

"That's cool," said Nat. He snatched the towel away from Tommy, the younger one, who was kind of nerdy looking. They both wore braces.

"We go to Dalton," said Nat. "Jeez, Tommy, this towel is soaked."

"Hey, man, get your own." Tommy shrugged at his brother.

"So is that gray-haired guy with your mom your grandfather or your dad?"

"He's our stepdad—I mean, our ex-stepdad," I said.

The boys looked confused and I couldn't blame them.

"Our real dad is dead," Robbie pitched in. I nodded.

We had decided after a few weeks at ASL, since we honestly had no idea where Daddy was or if we'd ever see him again, to cut off such discussions rather than try to deal with the series of confusing questions that would always follow statements like "We don't know where our dad is." The truth was that we had no real answers anyway and no place to go for them. Our dad was MIA, that was all we knew. I felt bad lying and sometimes worried that by lying it would come true to punish me—but it just seemed easier for everyone. Including me.

The boys nodded solemnly.

"You want to come to lunch? We've got a ton of beads." Tommy pointed at the outdoor restaurant at one end of the pool. Nat nodded in agreement.

"Sure," we said. After lunch, Robbie and I agreed to meet them for surfing lessons at the beach the next morning. None of us ended up being that good at it. The boys said the waves were puny anyway. We laughed and joked about being city kids.

"Nat and I were thinking maybe we could meet you down at the beach tonight when it's dark, you know, after dinner." Tommy shook his wet head.

I looked at Robin and we nodded. "Sure, see you then." We wouldn't have any trouble sneaking out.

That night after dinner in the hotel restaurant, Mother

and Pop went off on a rented scooter to experience Moroccan nightlife. I thought they looked comical with their helmets on, Mother clinging to Pop's bearish midsection, looking panicked in her safari suit and white Gucci pumps. Pop, decked out in Levi's and a denim jacket, revved the engine to scare her. As I looked at them, the difference in their ages seemed more pronounced to me now. He had gone all gray and wore a woolly Ernest Hemingway beard. She was the same, her beautiful self. Off they went, Mother shrieking as Pop peeled out of the club driveway.

Robbie and I walked down to the beach, looking around in the dark. There was a flashlight beam under a palm tree.

"Nat? Tommy? Is it you?" The ocean drowned out the sound of our voices.

Then Nat put the flashlight under his chin so that it lit up his face in a creepy way. "Ooooooo," he said, making a ghoul face.

Tommy grabbed the flashlight and they started fighting over it. "Give it!" Tommy said. We ran over to them and fell down onto the sand under the tree.

"What do you want to do?"

"I brought an empty 7UP bottle." Nat held it up. "We could play spin the bottle."

"Oh, yeah," Robbie said. I giggled.

"So who wants to go first?" Nat asked. There was a silence, then Nat said quickly, "Okay, I'll go."

We smoothed out the sand and sat in a circle. Nat placed the bottle down. On the first spin it pointed to Tommy.

"Hey, no way am I kissing you." Tommy guffawed. We all laughed. I nervously wondered who was going to get kissed first. The bottle spun again and pointed at Robbie. I felt a shiver of disappointment.

Robbie lifted her face up, going in for the lip-lock, when suddenly gunshots rang out over our heads. Instinctively, we all ducked down, only to be hit with a huge searchlight beam and then surrounded by men in burnooses armed with rifles yelling in French.

"*Halte!* Stop! *Cette zone est interdite!*" they shouted.

Squinting in the intense light, we all raised our hands like we'd seen in the movies. More men rode up on horses. They had rifles, too. Combining all our years of French to aid in translation, we figured out that the beach was off-limits at night and had to be patrolled to keep away the boats with drug runners on them.

"Oops," said Robbie, her eyes wide.

"*Pardonnez-nous, s'il vous plaît,*" uttered Nat meekly.

Tommy, scared shitless, was crying, ropes of snot coming out of his nose. "Omigod, they were gonna kill us," he choked out.

"*Qu'est-ce que vous faites ici?*" the men demanded.

"*Nous sommes désolées, messieurs,*" I whispered.

The men then smiled, lowering their weapons and patting us on our heads, as if we were lost children. It then occurred to me that I had peed in my pants. We stumbled back to the hotel and went straight to our rooms, where Robbie and I sat watching Moroccan TV in French.

"I can't believe I didn't get to kiss Nat," Robbie pouted.

"Yeah. Too bad." Of course, I was happy because she hadn't.

When Pop couldn't find what he was looking for, we said a sad good-bye to the boys, regretting the kisses we never got to have, and headed off across the Atlas Mountains in the washing-machine car. After a dusty drive with many goat and camel sightings, we arrived at the eleventh-century walled city of Marrakech. Always a famously exotic city, Marrakech, in the late sixties and early seventies, was a symbol of every Westerner's romantic, hashish-fueled dreams of North Africa.

We checked into the best hotel in the city, La Mamounia, just inside the city walls. La Mamounia was a rose-colored stone palace that had been built in the 1920s by a prince; it was surrounded by a lush two-hundred-acre garden. My sister and I had a room with a terrace that looked out over the agaves and bougainvillea and the palm, olive, and Savoy orange trees that surrounded the hotel.

With Mother and Pop we walked through the twisty streets of the city, with three or four children hanging on each arm, begging for money. Moving like a big protozoan, we toured Jamaa el Fna, the enormous square with snake charmers, chained monkeys doing tricks, and camels and donkeys for sale. From there we went to the souk, where the blue- and red-colored yarn dyed for carpets hung to dry on racks suspended over our heads. We visited the famous Koutoubia Mosque and the tombs of the Saadian, where the sultans are buried with their wives and children. Then we went back to the hotel and swam in the pool with Petula Clark's children.

"Go make friends with those blond girls," Mother had urged as she narrowed her eyes, scoping out the situation. While Mother pretended to take pictures of us while we cavorted in the pool with our new friends, she was really photographing Petula Clark's handsome Swiss husband, who was playing Marco Polo with us.

At dinner, we ate pigeon pie spiced with cinnamon, but only after Mother assured us it wasn't the kind of pigeon you saw in Trafalgar Square. Pop laughed and ordered another bottle of French wine. The waiters sprinkled lavender-scented water on our hands at the end of the meal. We were like any happy family on an exotic vacation.

Then, Mother ran into an old flame from New York in the lobby, Eliot Wyden, and greeted him too affectionately for Pop's liking. Mother had considered marrying Eliot for a brief time after her divorce from Pop. But problems arose when it turned out Eliot's mother disapproved of a multiple divorcée saddled with two children. Mother decided that she couldn't be married to a man who still cared what his mother thought, and besides, she didn't want to give up her alimony.

"Good Lord, Georgann, what are you doing here, of all places?" Eliot wetly kissed her cheek and thrust his big, floppy hands into the pockets of his Brooks Brothers blazer. I had always thought Eliot looked like a thumb. He was somewhat featureless and hairless.

"How is your mother, Eliot?" Mother was trying to postpone introducing Pop and wondering how to do so.

"She's dead!" Eliot blustered cheerfully. "Hit by a taxi last year crossing Madison."

"How awful. I'm so sorry," Mother said, her eyes sparkling the way Holly Golightly's did when she met Rusty Trawler, the richest man in America under forty.

"I would love to take you to dinner."

Mother laughed, looking over her shoulder at Pop. It was a tempting offer.

"Why don't you call me, Eliot, when you get back to the city?"

Pop looked furious and stomped off to the bar.

From that moment on, our meals together were either heavy with silence or fraught with sniping comments from the up-until-then happy couple. Robbie and I were on Pop's side. It seemed to us that if Mother was sleeping in the same room with Pop, she shouldn't flirting with some old boyfriend, or anyone for that matter.

One morning, Mother and Pop didn't show up for breakfast. I went up to their room and knocked on the door. A little, round Moroccan woman in a pink maid's uniform answered the door. She said nothing to me, but turned and went back to her work. The maid knelt on the white carpet, scrubbing at a dark stain. I noticed that a pane of glass in the French window that led out to the terrace was broken. A brown trickle led from the window to the bathroom. I could see blood on the sink and on some towels on the floor.

The maid looked up at me, clearly unhappy with the mess she had to clean up. I could hear my heart inside my head.

"*C'est du sang. Très difficile à enlever.*" She shook her head and clucked her disapproval.

I was trying to stay calm and guess what might have taken place at the same time. "*Où sont ma mère et mon père, madame, s'il vous plaît?*"

"*À l'hôpital, mademoiselle.*" She said something about an accident.

"*Merci, madame.*" I raced downstairs to the lobby, where I literally ran smack into Mother, looking as if she'd been up all night. She lifted a trembling hand up to her sunglasses and pushed them closer to her face. I searched her face and wrists but saw no blood or bandages.

"What's happened? Where's Pop?"

"He's fine. We had an argument, that's all." I followed her into the bar, where she ordered a bullshot—a 1970s pick-me-up like a Bloody Mary, but made with beef bouillon.

"But I saw your room," I whispered, standing next to her barstool, my eyes adjusting to the dark room.

"He punched his fist through the window. He was jealous about Eliot. He'd been smoking hash that he got somewhere. Thank God it's all over now. Jesus, what a night."

Mother lifted the salt-rimmed martini glass to her lips and sucked it down in one go. She then explained to me that even though Pop had no plans to leave his current wife, he didn't want her seeing other men and she had no intention of just being his mistress. So, they had reached an impasse and the deal was off. As a consolation prize, he had agreed to take out a life insurance policy in her name. This seemed to please her. She tapped on her glass, signaling the bartender for another. I didn't understand adults. And suddenly I wasn't so sure I wanted to be one.

Despite her numerous dalliances with men and women, many of them wealthier and younger than Pop, something special about him kept her coming back. And despite cheating on her, marrying one of her girlfriends, and possessing the means and the charm to capture any number of other women, Pop couldn't leave Mother for good. Maybe she saw him as a lover and a father; maybe he saw her as the classic doomed beauty in need of a savior. I'd read enough Jacqueline Susann to guess at these motivations, but at fourteen I couldn't possibly know. All I was sure of was that once again they had blown it—dangled a shiny idea of some kind of stable life for Robbie and me and then smashed it and left it for the maid to clean up.

I walked out of the tomblike darkness of the bar and into the Magritte blue of the Moroccan sky, where my bikini-clad sister lay on a chaise reading *Seventeen* magazine by the pool, looking like Sue Lyon sans lollipop in *Lolita*.

"So, where were they?"

"They had breakfast in their room," I lied. Despite Robbie's knowing-nymphet demeanor, I was still trying whenever possible to spare her the dirty details.

On our way home, Pop sat in the airport bar sullenly

drinking until our flight was called. I felt sorry for him. Sitting on his barstool, he seemed lost somewhere far away, like the little boy who had everything except the one thing he really wanted. Mother sat with us at a little café table, flipping through Italian *Vogue*, sipping white wine. She glanced over at him every couple of minutes, a faint smile curling up one side of her mouth.

After our return from Morocco, Tracy Turner came sashaying up to me in the hallway after gymnastics class.

"Hey, are you auditioning for the spring musical?" I noticed that she'd got blond streaks in her hair over the break, making her look even more like Farrah Fawcett.

"I don't know, are you?" I asked.

"Yeah, I thought it would be fun. Wanna go to the tryouts together?"

"Sure." We ran down the hall to sign up for a time slot. The show was *Bye Bye Birdie*, a zany 1960s show about an Elvis-type crooner who's drafted into the army. I was too afraid to sing at the audition but got cast in a nonsinging role as a kooky old lady, Mrs. Peterson, in a pillbox hat with my hair sprayed gray. Tracy played one of the cute bobby-soxers, in a ponytail, saddle shoes, and a poodle skirt.

Being onstage, even in a small part, was an amazing experience. I recognized that wonderful smell and breathed it in deeply—it took me back to the days at the Guthrie, and North Carolina, and of course my father. Acting became a way to be with him, to bring his faint memory back. The performing part was new and a bit difficult at first. I was always a little nervous before stepping onto the stage, but once I got out there, I found it exhilarating. I felt right at home, and my nerves vanished. I absolutely adored it and decided I would keep doing it, no matter what part I'd have to take.

A couple of shows later, I had a bigger part and acted with Lauren Bacall in the audience. We were doing *Inside a Kid's Head*, and her son Sam Robards played my boyfriend.

Mother came to see me for the first time and brought Yul, the polo player. When they came backstage afterward, Mother was in a low-cut, sexy Givenchy black dress and Yul wore his dirty jodhpurs and riding boots fresh off his horse, looking like an ad for a men's cologne. Even Lauren Bacall was staring at them and wondering if the glamorous couple were special "somebodies." Through the years I would gradually become accustomed to being upstaged by Mother, but it was Lauren Bacall who made me first realize Mother hadn't come to the play just to see me—she had come to be seen. And everybody looked.

Even though she experienced excitement and adventure partying all over Europe, Mother still craved more attention. The flame that was kindled at the trailer park, back when she was a small-town celeb in the local paper, still burned.

Encouraged by her singer friend, Marian Montgomery, Mother began to dabble with writing again—songs this time. Working together, they composed a song that Marian sang on the BBC. Mother was thrilled when we watched Marian on the telly, in a long, white, fluffy dress, and a picture hat, sitting in a swing, singing their song "Summerhouse."

Through Marian, Mother met the film director Silvio Narizzano and his lover, Win Wells, who was an actor, writer, and Silvio's muse. Mother instantly bonded with Win because he was from Kansas City. He was very flamboyant, dressed in tight, pastel-colored trousers and flowered shirts, unbuttoned to the navel. Silvio was more refined and classy, in jeans and a tweed coat. Win and Silvio wore wedding rings and would sometimes have horrible fights at our flat. Robbie and I would hear them screaming at one another in the living room—a crazy blizzard of curses and epithets.

"Bastard! What are you? Some kind of sadist!" Win would scream at the top of his lungs. Robbie and I would give each other the "uh-oh" look and settle in for the storm.

"Calm down, darling!" Silvio would shout.

"Calm down! I never want to see you again!"

"Boys! Please!" Mother would yell. "I can't hear myself think!"

At some point Win or Silvio would throw his wedding ring across the room or out the window. When, inevitably, they made up, Robbie and I would be called upon to hunt for the ring underneath furniture or out in the street.

Silvio's most well-known movie was *Georgy Girl*, but when Mother hooked up with him, he and Win were collaborating on a movie script, to be shot at their house in Andalusia. They wanted Mother and Marian to write some songs for it. Dennis Hopper was starring, along with Carroll Baker, Richard Todd, and Win in a small part.

In the script, there was a scene in which a bullfighter dies by being anally impaled by a bull in the ring. In another scene, a nun was devoured by cats. Carroll Baker's character, a faded movie queen named Treasure, was to sing Mother's song as she drowned in a fountain during a wild party. These peculiarities didn't faze Mother; her talents were in demand.

"I'll be back in a few weeks, girls. Don't forget to brush your teeth, and do your homework," she said as she climbed into a hired car Silvio had sent for her. She flew to Spain, scribbling away en route, and we were left to fend for ourselves, which at fourteen and fifteen we'd already been doing for quite some time. Mother called to check on us periodically from the set—which sounded to us like a dozen orgies all going on at the same time.

"What's that noise, Mother?" Robbie and I held the phone between us, trying to hear her over the din.

"Oh, that's Dennis overturning the drinks cart—he has the most violent temper!" Mother exclaimed.

Dennis Hopper was out of his gourd on an array of pharmaceuticals for most of the shoot, which led to numerous violent outbursts, and an erratic, often glazed acting performance. It wouldn't matter in the end because all the film stock was seized by the Spanish censors and banned for being obscene. Originally called *Las Flores del Vicio*, it found its way to drive-ins and video in the late seventies under the title *Bloodbath* and feels like a loopy cross between Buñuel and Hammer horror.

Soon after Mother's return to London, bombs started going off again all over the city courtesy of Fergus's old pals, the IRA. It was the third year of their campaign, but Mother was riding high off the hype surrounding the movie and not paying that much attention to anything but her lunch dates at San Lorenzo, or her latest fling. She had never taken the bombing seriously, so neither did we. Robin and I treated it like a game: we'd hear a bomb go off, run down to the local fish-and-chip shop for sustenance, and hop on the bus or into a taxi to look for the blast site.

This all seemed perfectly normal to me and good fun. It was like an episode of *Mission: Impossible* where I was Barbara Bain sitting in the back of the car twisting the window handles, pretending it was a safe that I had to open before we reached the target, and Robbie was Lesley Ann Warren secretly talking to headquarters through her Bonne Bell Lip Smacker.

When two separate bomb scares were phoned in to my school, the building had to be evacuated, but I didn't worry—none of us did. For a bunch of American kids who'd been carted from Cambodia to Syria to Venezuela, it was kind of like a snow day. We just went to the pub.

One morning we were sitting at breakfast with Mother in our little kitchen, which looked out on a lovely rose garden, the back wall of which abutted our tube station, Sloane Square. She was perusing a map of Devon and drinking tea.

"Tristan wants to take us down to Torquay this weekend." Tristan was her current squeeze—a real toff Englishman who was so upper class Robin and I couldn't understand a word he said. He'd open his mouth and what came out sounded like "Faw faw faw faw." He wore a bowler and carried an umbrella and seemed fairly harmless. Mother was also seeing a married TV actor ten years her junior named Terrence, but, understandably, only part-time.

"Are we staying in a hotel?" asked Robbie as she bit savagely into her sausage.

"Mmmm. It's called the English Riviera, Torquay."

"The beach. That sounds fun."

I eyed Robbie for talking with her mouth full.

"Isn't it time for you girls to go to school?" Mother was tracing the map with her finger. Suddenly we heard this incredibly loud sound—like a gigantic tin can bursting from the pressure inside. We turned to look out the window. From behind the back wall of our garden a huge fountain of orange flame shot up into the air. It vanished almost instantly, and black smoke started churning up into the sky. I heard loud shouts and a woman screamed. Robbie's sausage-filled mouth hung open, and Mother's teacup clattered onto its saucer. As we watched pieces of rock and shards of twisted metal fall into the garden and land on the grass in steaming lumps, Mother lit up a Dunhill. Her hands were shaking.

"Perhaps I should drive you two to school today," she said softly.

That September a bomb went off in the lobby of the London Hilton, where Mother's chum Mary Broomfield worked. Poor Mary was blown across the room, but the tourist she had been talking to was killed, and all that was left of her desk was a small briquette of charred wood. The explosion caused Mary to go deaf for a few days, and Mother put her in our guest room while she recovered. We brought her cups of tea and industrial-size scotches, both of which she lapped up happily. Even after her horrible ordeal, she remained cheerful, exhibiting true British pluck.

At Christmas, the IRA set off a bomb in Oxford Circus, shattering the windows of Selfridges department store. I had got my ears pierced there on the ground floor just six months before on my fifteenth birthday. Now there were gaping holes where the holiday windows had been and the street was covered in broken glass. The whole neighborhood was empty at a time when everyone was usually bustling about, doing their shopping at Marks & Spencer and the other stores. It cast an eerie pall on the season. Even as the bombs seemed to be getting closer, they didn't stop Mother from enjoying the holidays. We barely saw her on Christmas and only once or twice during the week. On New Year's Eve, Mother was going to a party in Holland Park. She headed out the door, reeking of Fracas, fishing in her bag for her car keys.

"I'm off. Be good. I'll be home late."

The door shut and she was gone. What were we going to

do? The only thing on telly was *The Bridge on the River Kwai*, and the shops were closed, so we sat in front of the electric fire and moped.

Then Robin sat up. "Hey, what about having our own party?" she suggested slyly. "I mean, everyone's folks are out getting blasted, right?"

"You're a genius," I said. We grabbed the phone and made some calls. Within half an hour, kids filled the house while T. Rex blasted from the stereo. The Cassidy girls showed up with a pack of people. Graham Becker, who was a senior, took up a collection and ran down to the off-license to buy beer. And soon, Tracy arrived with her coterie of hangers-on and admirers.

"Wow, great party, Wendy and Robin. Thanks for inviting us," Tracy said in her customary twang. All the boys' heads whipped around as she strode coltishly into the room. Someone turned out the lights and there were screams and cheers. While kids were dancing in the front room, I went outside to the garden, where people were smoking.

"It's bloody freezing," said Graham Becker, who had returned from the off-license with the goods.

"Let's make a fire," I suggested. "Everyone collect sticks and stuff, okay?" Soon we had a flimsy pile of twigs, leaves, and bits of wood from the tube station bombing in the center of the garden. Graham used his Zippo to light it. It mostly smoked.

"Hey," Graham said, "what else you got around here to burn?"

"I found something!" Lynn dragged a busted wooden chair out of a shed in the back of the garden. It was then that I realized she was wearing my mother's black Pucci cocktail dress with the tasseled belt and her leopard hat. T. Rex continued to blare through the back windows. Lynn tossed the chair on the fire, and it finally caught. The flames shot up into the evening sky and everyone whirled around them to the pulsating music.

I raced up the stairs and discovered Robbie had thrown open Mother's closets to the party, and half-naked girls were stripping off to try on her stuff. A few boys stood on the landing watching and laughing. Lynn's sister, Diane, was in a turquoise Moroccan caftan, draped in red Berber bead jewelry. Tracy was putting on a black wool jumpsuit that tucked into her boots and made her look like Emma Peel. Robin was wearing a Gucci leather gaucho outfit with an Hermès scarf wrapped around her head Gypsy-style, and most of Mother's jewelry. She saw me and handed me my favorite— a black Chanel toreador jacket with a matching flat hat. I grabbed a fox-fur coat, too, and headed out to the fire, followed by the other dress-ups. The fire needed more fuel, so I found some slats from a bed frame and a few dresser drawers in the shed to chuck on the burning pile. Dancing flamenco-style around the fire, clapping and whooping, banging our beer cans together, we looked like refugees from some fabulous swinging-London fashion-runway pub crawl. The air throbbed with David Bowie singing "Rebel Rebel," and we all sang along with him, our breath making clouds in the night air above us: "You've torn your dress, your face is a mess . . . we like dancing and we look divine."

As everyone strutted like hot tramps, I saw the flash of a lamp going on in the window upstairs. I looked up and saw Mother's face in the window. My blood turned to ice in my veins. She wasn't supposed to be there, in the window; she was supposed to be at a party and home late. But there she was, looking at us from behind the glass, her face frozen like that of Mrs. Danvers in *Rebecca* when Manderley is burning.

Out of the corner of my eye, I saw Robbie in mid-cavort suddenly stop and look up at Mother, her eyes bugging out in terror. "Holy crap!" she said.

"Quick, get the hose." I grabbed Graham Becker. "Put out the fire." He nodded his head, like it was no big deal, as if I'd asked him to put out his cigarette.

When I got to the living room, Tristan, the toff, was sitting in an armchair nursing a large brandy, and Mother's younger actor boyfriend, Terrence, was standing in the doorway surveying the scene. Mary Broomfield was also there, looking dazed in the dim light. I raced up to Mother, who was at the drinks tray, helping herself and Mary to hefty gins. Mother didn't turn to look at me as she spoke.

"I don't want to embarrass you in front of your friends, so I'll give you fifteen minutes to clear this lot out of here."

"I'm sorry, we should have asked if—"

"Asked if you could invite half the school here, if you could wear my best clothes, if you could drink alcohol?" Mother handed Mary her gin.

"My! Wendy! Don't you look smart!" Mary shouted, her hearing still affected by the London Hilton bomb. She drained her gin. "I'll have another, Georgie! Thank you!" She handed her tumbler to Mother. "Remember, no ice, dear!"

"What happened at your party?" I asked Mother.

"It was boring and the boys wanted to leave."

Tristan got up and helped himself to another drink.

"This is entertaining, Georgann. Fun to watch the young people."

Mother gave him a hostess smile, but I thought I could see a little steam coming from her ears.

Then, Terrence, who was a bit famous from being on the BBC and devilishly handsome, joined the sway of the party and drifted into a dance with Tracy. Tracy, a siren at fifteen, would later date Roman Polanski and become a B-movie star. She twisted her arms up in the air and smiled at him, doing her best Diana Rigg. He smiled back and took her in his arms, dipping her back until she screamed with laughter. The room was dimly lit and filled with bodies, and Mother's boyfriend was dancing with my girlfriend.

Tristan raised his glass and said, "May I wish everyone a very happy 1976!" Then he grabbed my hand and led me out onto the floor. "I say, may I have this dance?"

I smiled. He really wasn't so bad, I thought.

"I'm afraid not, Tristan," Mother said. "It's time for everyone to go home."

She went to the light switch and snapped it on. There was a collective groan. People began picking up their coats and handbags. Girls stripteased up the stairs, undoing the zippers and buttons on Mother's dresses and jackets on their way.

And there, in the too-bright light, I saw Mother looking at me as if she didn't recognize me, as if I were a stranger Tristan had brought with him and she were seeing me for the first time. She had turned her head away for what seemed like an instant—and Robbie and I had grown up and now we were women. And, I could see in her eyes, something even worse than that—we were competition.

It was then that Mother decided that the time had come for us to return to America.

chapter seven

BACK IN THE USA

Our return to the States was complicated by the news that my grandfather was dying of lung cancer. We hadn't been in New York a day when Mother announced we were going to Kansas City. It wasn't sentiment that drove her, it was money. We were broke. Mother had burned through her divorce settlement, paying off her giant credit-card tab, and all we had to live on was alimony. She needed to put in an appearance before the old man corked off.

Grandfather considered his daughter to be a fiscally irresponsible bubble brain who had married not one but two men who didn't have real jobs. If my mother had considered marrying my wealthy stepfather as an investment strategy, my grandfather was not impressed. Grandfather was a self-made man who had built a bank in Kansas City from the ground up. To him, my stepfather was a ne'er-do-well whose only understanding of money was how to spend it.

Thirty-six hours after walking out of our town house in South Kensington, Robbie and I sat on a plastic-covered couch in the large house in Kansas City, drinking Lipton instant iced tea and watching reruns of *To Tell the Truth* while Grandfather wheezed and grumbled from his La-Z-Boy recliner and his housekeeper, Louella, fussed over him. Mother sat on one of the antique carved wooden chairs Grandfather had brought back from China before World War II, chain-smoking Dunhills and chain-drinking California Chablis.

"Now, Mr. McAdams, let's try a little of this applesauce." Louella held the spoon up to Grandfather's lips, but he waved it away.

"Godammit, get that crap away from me. You're making me miss my favorite show."

Grandfather was usually in a foul mood, but dying made him really cranky. He seemed to hate all people, and Robin and I were terrified of him.

"Oh, Georgann, I just wish I could get some food into him," Louella mewed to my mother.

But Mother wasn't listening. I could see her eyes darting about, taking mental inventory of all my grandfather's more valuable possessions. There were some expensive rugs, paintings, and lacquered screens from China, as well as some big silver serving pieces and pretty cloisonné boxes. She popped a few of these into her handbag when she thought no one was looking, as if they were ashtrays from the Ritz.

While Mother's crusty, old relatives shuffled in and out to call on the dying man, they took turns ogling us as if we were circus freaks or ex-cons. Mother's uncle Darby asked her if her cigarette had "maryjawanna" in it.

"Why no, Darby. It's an English cigarette. Would you care to try one?" Mother replied demurely, and offered him the box.

He looked at it as if it were a severed head, and I could tell he didn't believe her. She was a fancy-pants woman not to be trusted.

Darby's wife, Aunt Elizabeth, brought Robin and me a tray of crackers with spray-on cheese, cocking her head to one side to show how much she pitied us. It was as if she were saying, "You poor lambs who have the Whore of Babylon for a mother, I know it's not much, but I brought you some snacks."

"Can I get you girls a refill on your iced tea?" Aunt Elizabeth asked as she leaned down with the tray.

"No, thank you." We politely took a cracker each; neither of us had ever seen cheese that came out of a can.

"Where did you get that pretty blouse, Miss Robin?" Aunt Elizabeth's eyes twinkled at the thought of her own kindness.

"I think it came from Madrid, Aunt Elizabeth." Robin looked down at her flowered shirt and peeled her legs off the plastic-covered couch to recross them.

On the side table was a photo of Robin and me sitting on the exact same couch dressed in our Easter best with our baskets. We were three and four and our little legs peeked out from under our dresses in white socks and Mary Janes.

"Oh, dear, that is far away, isn't it?" Aunt Elizabeth clucked. She had only been as far as St. Louis, on her honeymoon, and imagined Europe as a large opium den filled with communists and clothing-optional resorts.

When it was time to go, Mother steered us over to the La-Z-Boy to kiss Grandfather's papery cheek good-bye.

"What are you always kissing me for?" he groused, wiping our kisses away with the back of his hand. He died a few weeks later.

The Death Watch visit ended up being only semi-successful; Grandfather did leave Mother some money, but left the house and its contents to his loyal housekeeper, Louella, who Mother said was a hillbilly. This was a crushing blow to Mother, who felt that she was being denied not only what was rightfully hers, but any reparation for her horrific childhood. For her, it was the ultimate rejection from the only father she had ever known.

With the rest of the money, Grandfather had set up small trust accounts for me and my sister to pay for college, most likely knowing that there would be no money for us if it was anywhere Mother could get her hands on it. Of course, this made Mother even more furious, and she proved him correct when, in an extreme act of retail therapy, she tried to salve the wounds of her father's betrayal with a chocolate-brown Mercedes sedan with tan leather upholstery—purchased in cash.

The trusts were buried at the bank in Kansas City, and we would inherit them when we turned twenty-one. Mother periodically reminded me that the money in our trust accounts was really hers, and that she fully expected us to turn it over to her as soon as we came of age.

After Kansas City, we set up temporary residence at a Howard Johnson's in Danbury, Connecticut, and Pop reappeared like the genie from the lamp and started driving Mother around to look at houses. He had divorced Mother's girlfriend and thought two ex-wives in the city was enough. Mother had burned too many bridges there anyway, so they both decided some cozy little Yankee enclave a short trip away in the bar car seemed like a good idea. She even liked the names of the towns: Milford, Greenwich, Darien. How long it would last this time with Pop, I didn't know. We still loved him, but Robbie and I decided after Morocco that they would never get back together permanently, so we kept our investment in the relationship to a minimum.

After two months at the HoJo's, Mother found a house she liked—a rented white farmhouse with a stone wall around it in Ridgefield. It was a charming house in a tastefully understated New England town with a main street and a white gazebo in the town square. Every time I rode my bike I expected to see Betsy Ross on her front porch churning butter and waving the flag or something.

Mother started making us sack lunches and walking us to the bottom of the road where the school bus picked us up. It was the new her: the gracious Connecticut Yankee

Housewife, minus the annoying husband. The sort of persona Martha Stewart would later perfect, package, and turn into a fortune.

As Mother walked back into her Pepperidge Farm commercial, the bus would take us to Ridgefield High, where Robin and I stuck out like a two-headed baby. The kids thought we were snobs because we talked funny and had been (compared to them) everywhere. When someone asked me where I'd got my sweater, I made the mistake of telling her Paris. We were freaks of the highest order, and good students, too, which was an even greater crime than owning a French sweater. It wasn't my fault that I did my homework on time and didn't own a pair of painter's pants or a Kiss T-shirt. It seemed fruitless to even try to fit in, so we didn't. We walked up and down the locker-lined halls together, shoulder to shoulder, chins up, and eyes straight ahead, daring anyone to mess with us while praying they wouldn't.

While we were the unhappy pariahs at the high school, Mother started cheerily seeing men she met around town. Bob, who ran the service station and had a shaved head à la Telly Savalas, picked her up at the town newsstand. A man named John crawled up our driveway and let the air out of her tires when she broke up with him. And there was Tom, a slick dude in a shiny blue suit whom Mother described as her "lawyer."

To shield Robbie from the frequency and rapacity of Mother's sex life, I had become an expert at covering up the fact that she had one. In London, the gentleman sleeping in the guest room was easy to explain, but back in the States Mother became a little sloppier at hiding her affairs, so I would sneak upstairs to hide a suit jacket or big shoes before my sister had a chance to see them. Sometimes I failed. Once, Robbie and I had just got home from school when I heard her cry out in distress. I dropped my backpack and ran to her room. She was standing in front of a wicker chair, upon which hung Tom's trousers.

"Omigod, omigod! Whose are those? What are they doing here?" She was fifteen and totally grossed out.

"I'm sure there's a perfectly logical explanation." I tried to look nonchalant.

"Eeeew! That's soooo nasty!" She jumped up and down, clawing at her throat as if she were gagging. "You don't think Mother did anything in my bed, do you?" Her voice started sounding tighter and higher as her mind started to form a picture of an act too revolting to contemplate—Mother and some naked guy cavorting on her blue-flowered bedspread underneath her poster of Jim Morrison. The years of trying to protect Robbie had steeled me against it. To me, Mother's sex life was annoying, and inconvenient. For Robbie, just the idea of it was disgusting.

"Of course not. What, are you kidding?" I put my hands on my hips, trying to look professorial. "Whoever's they are, he probably just spilled something on them and had to put on another pair." This sounded asinine as it came tumbling out of my mouth, but, incredibly, she bought it.

"Really?"

It was because she wanted to think it was true, like when you're too old to believe in Santa Claus and the tooth fairy but you cling to the last shred of innocence you still possess.

"Sure."

Even though Robbie and I had the Happy Hooker for a mom, we were fairly ignorant when it came to sex. Mother had neglected to inform us of the basics—maybe she was too busy in the advanced course.

We met Tom a week later when he came to pick Mother up for a dinner date. I thought lawyers had to wear their pants, but it seemed Tom didn't always need his. Mother got rid of him when he suggested a three-way with her and my sister.

I don't know if it was all the fresh country air or making the sack lunches or the boyfriends' scarpering, but it didn't take long for the cracks to appear in her June Cleaver façade. Mother, who up until then had always been a well-groomed and impeccably dressed size 4, gained fifteen pounds, stopped going to the hairdresser to get her hair frosted, and stopped changing her clothes, preferring to remain in her nightgown all day.

The years of shopping, dancing, and glamour in London had somehow kept the pin in the grenade of Mother's psyche, but now it was out and she blew up, went nuts.

She bought an air rifle and started running out onto the porch like a frenzied cowpoke in a western and shooting at any dog or cat that came into our yard. The paper girl stopped coming, too afraid to venture into the crosshairs.

When Mother wasn't running around with a lit cigarette and a gun, she was locked up in her room for days at a time. When she did emerge, it was in the middle of the night and she was on a rage-fueled mission to destroy. It was the beginning of what Robin and I called *the warpath*.

"Wake up, both of you, this instant!" Mother would cry as she turned the overhead lights on in our rooms. Surprised at the suddenness and severity of these attacks, we were too afraid to get out of bed and just pulled the covers over our heads, rolled into balls, and waited for it to be over.

"You've ruined my life!" she'd scream as she overturned my bookshelf and ripped pictures from my walls. The tinkling of falling glass would play over her feet as she beat a path to my sister's room.

"I wish you'd been abortions!" she'd shout as she flipped the little table on which Robbie kept her music-box collection.

Then, as quickly as she had come, she was gone—screeching off like a banshee in her nightgown. The field of destruction would settle as the warbly wheezing of the music boxes playing "Twinkle, Twinkle, Little Star" or "Edelweiss" would slowly fade.

At first, Robbie tried to glue her music boxes back together, but she gave up eventually and just put all the little bits back up on the table. There was something very sweet and hopeful about her refusal to throw them away. Little chimneys and gates lay next to the bombed-out shells of what had once been a jaunty Alpine chalet or a cute carousel with elves riding on it. My sister's favorite one featured a bird, a robin, sitting on a picket fence. At one time it had played "I'd Like to Teach the World to Sing," but now it sounded like a backward, low-speed version of "Sympathy for the Devil." The bird's head had been snapped off and lost. Its body lay on the shelf, decapitated.

We quickly learned to hold our breath and read the signs when we trudged up the driveway in the snow after school. Were the lights on in the kitchen? Could we smell something cooking mixed with cigarette smoke? Was it safe? One day we returned home in the snow to find she had locked the front door.

"What should we do?" I looked through the window in the door into the dark kitchen. There were no signs of life.

"We have to break in," Robbie snapped, clearly ticked off at our dilemma, as well as our mother's lack of sanity.

"But if we break in, she'll get mad."

"Oh, who cares! Let her get mad! I'm freezing." Robbie picked up a big rock on the porch that we used as a doorstop and chucked it through the glass. Then she reached her arm over and turned the doorknob.

"There," Robbie said, swinging the door open for me. "She's so out of it, she probably won't even notice."

After nine months of this, we were so desperate I called Pop in New York. He was trying again to patch things up with his first wife, but he still came up to Connecticut to play fairy ex-stepfather.

On my sixteenth birthday he had given me a used Subaru

coupe and taken us all to see *A Chorus Line* on Broadway, followed by dinner at Sardi's. I'd thought the show was interesting. All the people in it were unhappy about something—they didn't like their bodies or they were ashamed of being gay or didn't feel loved by their parents. But they had been able to escape their problems, sort of, by becoming performers. I'd thought, was that why I liked acting? And was there a way for me to escape?

It hadn't been much of a celebration, as Mother had hated the show and spent most of it in the theater bar, sulking. She had complained sourly all through dinner. But Robbie and I were happy to be back under the dazzling lights and marquees of Broadway. The city was so alive and filled with people, not like Ridgefield, where it was dark at night and all you could hear were the insects rubbing their legs together.

After almost a year in Ridgefield, Pop was our only connection to our old, fun life. He was also the only person, maybe because of his money at least, who still had any influence on Mother, and the only father figure we had.

The phone rang and rang. Someone picked up after about the tenth ring.

"Pop?" I could tell by the wheezy breathing that it was him. I also heard the familiar sound of ice cubes in a glass.

"Yes, dearie."

"I was wondering if you could speak to Mother. She's been locked up in her room for days. And I think maybe she's been drinking a lot."

"Well, dearie, I'll try and talk to her, but you know your mother. . . ."

His voice trailed off. I wanted to say, *Well, I may know her, but I sure don't understand her.* But I didn't.

"Thanks," I said.

I don't know if Pop made the call, but she emerged from the miasma of her room in the spring and was somehow fine again. It was if she had woken from a long winter's nap and not a nervous breakdown, which was certainly one way of looking at it.

Robbie and I took advantage of her exit from lulu land and convinced her that this country-mouse life was making us all despondent. What we needed was new surroundings. We could move to Boston, which wasn't New York, and no one knew us there. Wouldn't that be fun? It would be like it used to be in London. She could make new friends, start going out again. It would be like old times.

And it worked, for a while.

BOSTON, 1977

chapter eight

PLAY DEAD

In Boston, just as she had in London, Mother zeroed in on the most happening and poshest neighborhood she could find. In the late seventies, that was Cambridge and, for us, a mansion for rent that stood behind a long, serpentine stone wall on Fresh Pond Parkway. It was a pile, with four bedrooms that all had interconnecting dressing rooms and loos, a sunken living room added in the twenties, a solarium, and an outdoor porch that hugged the entire back of the house, which looked out on a glorious lawn peppered with dogwood trees, their petals trembling and floating in the wind. While it was way out of our price range, Mother embraced living beyond our means, as usual. Locally famous as "the house behind the wavy wall," it and Pop's introductions got Mother almost instant invitations from Cabots and Lodges and many of the bright young things of the Boston literary and arts scene. Soon she was lunching at the Ritz at least once a week and had her own table at Harvest, a chic nouvelle-cuisine spot in Cambridge.

The house gave Robbie and me easy access to Harvard Square and a summer full of bright lights and fun distractions like we'd had in London and could only dream about during the long, dull nights and days in Ridgefield. We practically skipped along the streets of Cambridge, flipping through LPs at the Harvard Coop and shopping for long, flowered skirts, cowboy boots, and jumpsuits in Urban Outfitters. We went to movies at the Harvard Square Theatre or more often at the Brattle, a revival house featuring sophisticated and racy double bills like *The Boys in the Band* and *The Women*.

On weekends while Mother was partying with society trust-fund babies, Robbie and I would drive to the beach in Provincetown and eat boiled lobsters and corn on the cob out of foil-lined bags on the rocks. At sunset, we'd change in the Subaru and go out dancing in the gay bars in P-Town. Robbie was an expert at charming the bouncer at the door, and we always got in. No one ever bothered us, perhaps thinking we were together, and we'd dance our asses off until last call. Then, soaked in our own sweat, we'd stumble out into the street, to see Edward Gorey riding by on his bicycle like Ichabod Crane on wheels, and hunt for our car. I'd drive home and we'd listen to the radio. Robbie would put her bare feet up on the dashboard, and her hand with a cigarette would dangle out the window. If we passed someone on the road, she'd defiantly, and just for the fun of it, give them the finger, and we'd end up in a drag race with the offended driver of the other car—screaming with laughter and singing at the top of our lungs to the Police's "Roxanne" as we raced along the empty beach roads.

While we were gone on one of these Cape Cod expeditions, Mother met the next man of her dreams, Frank Collins, at the bar at Harvest.

Frank lived somewhere in Vermont with his wife and family and would visit Mother when he came to Boston on business. He was tall, thin, and blond and wore horn-rimmed glasses. It didn't seem to bother her that he was married, but it bothered me because I knew there was no chance he would marry her and take care of her so we wouldn't have to keep calling Pop to lend us money all the time.

I only had one conversation with Frank. During one of his lunchtime visits, he described tearing the wings off flies when he was a small child—apparently this was what he did for fun. As he told me this story, he smiled and looked really happy and my mother stared adoringly at him, as she did whenever he said anything.

The only other thing I knew about him was a story my mother had told me about his hitting a little girl accidentally with his car many years ago. The girl had darted out into the road, not giving him time to react or stop the car, and she was killed instantly. According to my mother, he felt terrible and would never recover from the horror of it. I wasn't sure I believed it was really an accident after hearing him talk about what he did to the flies.

He reminded me of a character in a John Cheever story,

someone who seems normal and nice, but underneath the calm façade there's all this darkness boiling that he barely contains with his flashing smile and perfectly polished shoes. Frank came and went suddenly, as if he had his own trapdoor in the floor. But Mother seemed happy when she was with him, and despite some bitchy moments, she wasn't on the warpath the whole time they saw each other.

Mother and Frank went off on little trips to Maine and Nantucket. She talked about how he was planning to leave his wife. I wanted to tell her not to hold her breath. I had done a little research on this in *Cosmo* and had discovered that a small percentage of men left their wives for other women. I decided to keep the information to myself, but at the same time I worried about Mother getting her hopes up. And I was worried, too, about who would be left holding the bag when things didn't work out.

And they didn't work out. Just like it said in *Cosmo*.

After stringing her along for six months and wining and dining her all over the Eastern Seaboard, Frank decided to stay with his wife. This tragedy, coupled with the alienation of some of her new crowd and another run on her finances, sent Mother into a period of black despair and us all into a slightly less grand house on top of a hill in Belmont, a leafy suburb of Boston. After the move, and Frank's betrayal, Mother was heartbroken and, like a Victorian lady in mourning, took to her bed. Only Mother's version of appropriate mourning attire was her blue Pucci nightgown. And instead of weeping and making bracelets from her departed beloved's hair, she chain-smoked and plotted a murder/suicide that would make the six o'clock news.

It was Thanksgiving, months later, when she came downstairs fully dressed for the first time. She had changed out of the nightgown into a tailored, brown Jaeger skirt and a pale pink silk blouse. One of her three pearl necklaces adorned her throat, and an Hermès scarf that perfectly matched her blouse was expertly placed over her shoulders, the knot settled on her chest. She had put her frosted blond hair back in a chignon and had even put on some makeup.

Mother set the table with her Limoges china and the Tiffany flatware that we hadn't seen since we'd left Park Avenue. She cooked a turkey with all the trimmings. Looking at her elegant appearance and the lovely table setting, I had to admit that when she wanted to, she could still pull it together. The trickier question was how long she could keep it up.

Robin and I sat at the table watching Mother carefully carve the turkey—our mouths hanging open ever so slightly as if we were witnessing a miracle. She placed the turkey slices on our plates and spooned mashed potatoes and green beans next to them. Then she heaped on the stuffing and, doing her best Donna Reed, said, "Help yourselves to the cranberry sauce." She pushed a stray strand of hair behind her ear with the back of her hand, just like a contented housewife.

"Thank you, Mother," I said, smiling. "Everything looks delicious." I looked at Robbie, cuing her to compliment

Mother's cooking, but she just stared back at me and said nothing.

In silence, we began pushing mashed potatoes onto our forks and spearing green beans. The clock ticked. The carving knife clicked against the serving fork.

I thought of how other people celebrated the holidays: laughing and joking with grandparents, cousins, and old friends. But not us, because we didn't have any. The house in Belmont was our tenth home in twelve years, and my mother had no more friends left, old or new, having driven them all away. Robbie and I had decided that this was her superpower, and we were too afraid to invite our friends over in case she turned it on them. So it was just the three of us, the turkey, and our cat Gus, a stowaway from Ridgefield, and I wasn't even sure how long he planned to stick around.

I was staring into my mashed potatoes, feeling sorry for myself, when Mother decided to ratchet things up a little by polishing off a bottle of Almaden Chablis in about five minutes flat. This was a trick she had perfected years before with a cold, crisp Pouilly-Fuissé, and although her finances had forced her to move on to the cheaper labels, the result was the same. Her empty glass tipped over onto the table and she moved back onto the warpath for the first time since we'd moved to Boston and she'd met Frank.

She fixed her woozy gaze upon us. Her eyes filled with a creepy intensity that made me feel as if she could see inside me to the knotted heap of fear that had replaced my stomach.

"Do you know something, Wendy and Robin?" Her voice was quiet with a touch of acidity from the cheap wine.

Here we go, I thought. The jungle drums were beating in the distance, the natives were coming to get us.

"I have sacrificed my whole life to raise the two of you."

My sister and I sat at the table frozen, our forks poised in midair. I was too afraid to look at her so I stared down at my dinner plate. I noticed that my gravy was running into my green beans. I hated that.

"My *whole* life." The drums were growing louder.

"No one else gives a *shit* about you." The natives were almost upon us.

"You're just selfish little *brats!*" She stood up and threw her napkin onto her plate of uneaten food. Stumbling back against her chair, in high dudgeon now, she raised her hand to her breast.

"You will *never* know how much I have given up because of the two of you!" she snarled.

My sister and I did not move, did not breathe. At least when she had raided our rooms at three in the morning, we had the covers to hide under. An icy tingling started to creep up the back of my neck and onto my scalp—an all too familiar feeling that never seemed to improve with time.

"'How sharper than a serpent's tooth it is to have a thankless child!'"

I can't remember exactly when, but somewhere between our evacuation from London, the Kansas City Death Watch, and the suburban nightmare of Ridgefield, she'd begun to quote Shakespeare or the Bible when things were about to get really hairy.

But before we could move, the *Mommie Dearest* routine was cut short by the wine or an act of God and she passed out and keeled over onto the carpet.

Robin and I looked at each other. Was she really out or was this just another lunatic, attention-getting ploy? It was Thanksgiving, for God's sake, and the food was getting cold.

"Maybe she's dead," Robin said. "Or faking it."

I looked under the table. Mother's chest was moving. "She's out cold."

Mother had often played dead through the years, though when we were seven and eight it was more a game than a tactic. She would ghoulishly limp to her bed and flop down on the mattress, and my sister and I would scream and jump on her, poking her and pleading with her to wake up. The game would always go on a little too long, my mother being very good at it, and we would start to really believe that she was dead. We'd lift her heavy arms and legs and drop them onto the bed wondering why she wouldn't move. Finally, after our fear overcame us, we'd start to cry, and it was only then that she would open her eyes, coming back to life at the sound of our tears. It was a kind of twisted version of the fairy-tale prince's kiss. It was her way of gently reminding us that she was all we had. If she were to die, we would have no one.

Robbie and I looked at each other and slowly got out of our chairs. We approached the body with great caution—

the way you would a dangerous animal you had just shot on safari that might suddenly spring back to life and leap up to tear your throat out.

"Mother?" I looked down at her and waited a full minute. Then I knelt on the carpet and poked her with my finger a few times. No response. "You'd better go call an ambulance," I said to Robbie.

"Shit," she said. "Happy Thanksgiving, we're going to the emergency room."

We opted to drive behind Mother's ambulance in our now battered Subaru; it was always important to have a get-away car in case . . . well, just in case. I drove because I was older and my sister was a bad driver, a Boston driver. Since getting her license four months before, she'd had so many accidents in the car that both doors were now fused shut and the only way to get in and out was to crawl through the windows. This always attracted attention whenever we arrived anywhere and made for a fairly spectacular entrance at the Mount Auburn Hospital, where we screeched into the parking lot behind the ambulance, crawled out of the windows, and rushed into the ER entrance.

Robin and I sat in the ER waiting room, and after about an hour, our mother's gynecologist, Dr. Stander—the only man she ever really trusted—arrived. It had started raining and his raincoat was wet and dripping onto the shiny waxed floor.

"Don't you girls worry," he said very reassuringly. He was very reassuring, like God with a mustache.

We smiled weakly at him, offering no information as none was needed.

"Your mother is a very sick woman," he said, leaning down to look into our eyes for emphasis. The television up on the wall behind his head gave him a kind of weird electric halo. Then, having nothing else to offer, Dr. Stander turned and ran through the ER's double doors, shedding his wet raincoat as he disappeared. My sister and I looked at each other. We were too old for this.

We sat in the waiting room and passed the time by playing one of our favorite games: Murder. We played it to comfort ourselves; we both knew that. Somehow, if only for a moment, it made us feel that we were in the driver's seat.

This time, we plotted the fabulously gruesome murder/death of the man we blamed for this most recent bout of Mother's suffering and insanity: Frank Collins. He had broken her heart by not leaving his wife and had made our lives a living hell, and he was going to have to pay. Things had been bad in the past, but whatever quality of life our move to Boston had returned to us had been stomped on by this asshole's big, tasseled loafers. We'd already endured weeks of coming home from school to a dark house with no food in the fridge, no dinner bubbling on the stove, and an empty baked-beans can on the counter with a big wooden spoon sticking out of it. And now, here we were in the ER on Thanksgiving. It sucked.

"Hey, remember that movie about the girl with those amazing psycho powers?" Robin asked me.

I stared at her jiggling foot and bit my nails. "*Psychic* powers, stupid. You mean *The Fury*." We had just seen it at the Harvard Square Theatre. "Starring Amy Irving and John Cassavetes, directed by Brian De Palma." I was beginning to consider myself a bit of a film buff.

"Yeah, well, remember when she made the blood come out of that guy's eyes and stuff? Wouldn't it be cool if we could make Frank's head explode into a million pieces like she did to that guy who really pissed her off at the end of the movie?"

I pictured Amy Irving's character totally losing it and blowing up the bad guy's head. It's pretty gross because it's in slow motion and you see parts of his head flying around the room.

"Yeah, that would be awesome." I imagined Frank's glasses being blasted off his face as his head detonated and chunks of him flying in slow motion through the air: a bloody ear and his thin upper lip floated by as we jumped up and down with glee as if we'd just won what was behind door number three on *Let's Make a Deal*.

The emergency room was fairly empty; maybe because it was Thanksgiving. Other people were home drinking hot chocolate and playing Scrabble after their festive holiday meal. Robin and I sat in chairs against the wall staring at the news on TV. The sound was turned down. The screen showed a huge fire that was burning somewhere downtown.

"Yeah, I'd love to see Frank's brains all over the curtains," I said dreamily.

"Or, we could just run him over with the Subaru," Robin said.

"Quick and easy." Vehicular homicide, it was almost too good for him.

"Yeah, and we're too young to go to jail, aren't we?"

Yes, we probably were, but jail didn't seem so bad to me now. It even sounded kind of . . . well, nice. I was sure there was a lot of structure and three meals a day.

After the news was over, Johnny Carson came on and we moved on to planning Mother's death—even though she was doing a pretty good job on her own. Since we had already used the car to kill Frank, we needed something new.

"Hey, I know. We could push her down the basement stairs," I said.

Robbie smiled. We always remembered the old bedtime story from the Dakota, partly because it was terrifying and partly because it was one of the few times Mother had actually told us a story at bedtime.

"We could do that. Get her to go down to the basement stairs and then do it," I said.

"Yeah," Robbie said. "We'll run Frank over first and then push Mother down the stairs."

After we played Murder, I went to get some Diet Pepsis and candy bars to celebrate everyone's being snuffed out and all our problems being solved. When I got back, Dr. Stander was waiting with Robin.

"Well, girls, it seems your mother will be staying the night and perhaps an extra day or two." He cocked his head to the side at us as if we were cute puppies. Mother had hemorrhaged internally due to an old IUD she had and would have to have a D&C in the morning. "Any questions?" He raised his eyebrows in anticipation.

I wondered how Mother could have claimed to have been pregnant last year by that Jewish architect and had an abortion if she had an IUD, but said nothing.

"Yeah, Dr. Stander, what's a D and C?" Robin asked, as if it were something you ordered at the Dairy Queen.

"Well, Robin, D and C stands for 'dilation and curettage'; it is surgery to treat abnormal uterine bleeding," he said, as if describing the changing of a tire. "Your mother is heavily sedated but you can come and see her tomorrow."

We headed back out to the parking lot. I handed Robbie the Snickers, which I knew she liked. "Happy Thanksgiving, Robbie," I said as I washed down my 3 Musketeers with some now room-temperature Diet Pepsi.

"Oh, yeah, you, too." She lit up a Parliament and took a huge drag. "Want one?"

"No, thanks. Hey, I bet the Pilgrims didn't have candy and soda on Thanksgiving."

She laughed. "Or Parliaments. You want me to drive?"

"No way."

We crawled into the Subaru and made our getaway.

The next morning I woke up and assessed the damage. The turkey was still on the table, along with the mashed potatoes, but our cat, Gus, had eaten most of the green beans, which he really loved. I was glad someone had a good time. I went into the kitchen to get a big garbage bag. Robin was heating up chicken-noodle soup for breakfast and smoking a cigarette.

"Want some soup?" She inhaled deeply, flicking the ashes onto the linoleum with her thumb.

She was wearing jeans with holes in the knees and a tight T-shirt, displaying what my mother liked to call her Rita Hayworth taste. The whole effect was very teenage runaway. Robin had fully evolved into the defiant one—she didn't care if Mother caught her smoking in the house or found out she had cut math class.

But I never stopped trying to be the dutiful daughter— always striving to do the right thing and make nice. I could be a real drag.

"Mother's going to kill you if she finds out you've been smoking in the house," I warned.

"Oooh, I'm terrified. Crackers?" She tossed a package of saltines onto the table, placed a bowl of soup down, and sank into the chair across from me. We slurped in silence.

After breakfast, we took out the trash and headed over to the hospital to see our mother. Unlike with Mother's first trip to the hospital, after she'd locked us in the closet for a day, when we arrived to visit at Mount Auburn, there were no moccasins and she didn't look like a fairy princess; she looked like shit. She was puffing away on a cigarette in her cigarette holder, defiantly blowing the smoke at the NO

SMOKING sign on the bilious green wall. We took turns kissing her cheek, then sat in the plastic chairs next to the bed.

"Mother, you look great," I said. She looked as if she would have sold one of us for a glass of white wine had there been a market nearby.

"They've taken out practically all my internal organs. It's a miracle I'm still alive," she snorted.

I turned to Robbie for backup, hoping that she would say something nice, but she just glowered and snapped her gum. I couldn't think of anything to say. There was nothing to say. Sitting there, I felt overwhelmed by a deep feeling of utter helplessness. It was like a black blob crushing me that made me wish I were dead. I couldn't do anything that would make things better. Our family, such as it was, was like a big dying animal. And there wasn't a shovel large enough to bury it, cover it up, or put it out of its misery.

After about ten minutes, my mother turned her face away from us. The audience was over.

"We'll go now, Mother," I said. "See you tomorrow."

I was afraid Robin was about to say something unhelpful so I grabbed her arm and dragged her away. It was best to get out before there was an eruption.

I admired Robin's fuck-you attitude, which was so different from anything I would ever dare to do. After years of trying to shield my sister from the truth, I had almost come to believe my little Girl Scout routine. When things were bad with Mother, whatever anger or resentment I felt was channeled into my cover-up. I still wanted the neighbors, everyone at school and at the grocery store, to think that we were just like everyone else. When things with Mother calmed down, I was just so grateful for the peace, I didn't want to do anything that would disturb it. Trying to disguise it all was my full-time job; and for a while, I thought I was fooling the world.

chapter nine

THE NEW AND IMPROVED GEORGANN

After Mother came home from the hospital, things went back to a strange version of the way they were when she wasn't on the warpath. She was up and dressed in the morning, making us toast with little, cold lumps of butter embedded in them and mugs of hot chocolate. Everything tasted like the inside of the refrigerator. She had a lit cigarette in an ashtray in every room in the house so she could just smoke from room to room like Tarzan swinging from vine to vine. We came home from school, and dinner was there, ready for us. My sister and I set the table, cleared the dishes, did homework, and watched TV. It was like we were the Waltons or something.

Since the fall after we'd moved to Boston, we attended Beaver Country Day School in Chestnut Hill, where I was a senior and Robin was a junior. Beaver was billed as a "college preparatory school" on the sign out by the stately front gate on Hammond Street. It was well-appointed, with soccer fields, tennis courts, and a swimming pool. Many of the kids came from well-to-do families, and the headmaster was kind of famous because he had taken Sylvia Plath to the prom. In short, the school had just the right country-club patina for Mother.

Beaver was our third school in three years. By now Robin and I were accustomed to being the new kids. It was our métier, and any novelty attached to it had worn off for us long ago. The important question had been, where would we fit in? Beaver had three basic cliques: the preppies, the jocks, and the stoners. Robin and I didn't qualify as members of any of those groups, so we gravitated toward the Drama Club—a kind of artistic catchall for the kids who didn't belong anywhere else. There was Sally Messman, who had a genius IQ, a mouthful of metal, and an unruly mop of black, curly hair. Neal Burch was a tall, hulking boy who lurched when he walked and had a bad lisp; "Athole," he would say to the kids who made fun of him. Mitch Hall, who wore the same blue jacket to school every day, was always trying to call the pope or Idi Amin on the pay phone in the student lounge.

This band of social pariahs was ruled over by the drama teacher, Mr. Valentine. A short, ruddy-faced man with flaming red hair, he wore plaid pants and turtlenecks instead of a suit and tie like the other male teachers. Some days he even wore a medallion. Mr. V was rumored to have had a nervous breakdown the term before we'd arrived at Beaver. His hands shook, supposedly because of the lithium he had been put on after the breakdown. This made him seem to us like some kind of tortured, tragic artist. He was a little angry and sarcastic and had a sinister laugh—he definitely had an edge. Mr. V's classroom was in a little house near the pool, a separate kingdom where he taught theater classes and held Drama Club meetings.

As soon as I started going to V's theater classes and to Drama Club meetings, I knew I had found my place. Since my first play in London, I had known that I loved to act. But what had started as a way to connect to my long-lost father had developed into something even more intimate. I loved pretending to be someone else; it was so much easier than being me. I could hide inside this other person and, even if just for a short time, inhabit a completely different world far away from the one I had to live in every day. And I was pretty good at it, or so other people seemed to think.

Another attraction Mr. V held for a group of disenfranchised teens like us was that he chose material that was basically inappropriate for high school students. The first play we had staged that fall was Lanford Wilson's *The Rimers of Eldritch*, which featured bestiality, adultery, elder abuse, and even had a rape scene. When the lights came up at the end of the play for curtain call, the cast was greeted by silence, as hundreds of parents stared, mouths agape, utterly appalled by the unwholesomeness of what they had just witnessed their little darlings doing onstage. The moment lasted a good fifteen seconds before Mr. V began stridently clapping. Slowly, the parents joined in, putting their hands together and looking at each other with embarrassment as if they all smelled a huge fart.

"Why can't they do *The Music Man* or *Ah, Wilderness!*, for Christ's sake?" I heard a dad complain after the show. It gave us all a thrill to shock the parents with our bold theatrical choices. I think V felt the same way. He got a big kick out of the dropped jaws at curtain call. He was our leader and a dangerous rebel.

After *The Rimers of Eldritch*, Mr. V announced that the next play the Drama Club would be performing was called *David and Lisa*.

"Okay, listen up," he barked, shuffling the mimeographed scripts in his small, chapped hands. "This is a play about two teenagers who meet in a residential treatment center and form a friendship that helps heal them as human beings."

"You mean like an insane asylum?" asked Mitch Hall, smiling. Mitch was our technical director; he built sets and always ran the lights. He had recently caused quite a stir by frying an egg on the light board to show it was dangerous and outdated.

"No, more like a high school for troubled kids who don't get to go home at the end of the day. Neal, you will be playing David, who is obsessed with cleanliness and hates to be touched."

"I thee," lisped Neal. His hair always hung in his face and hid his acne.

"Sally, you will be playing Lisa, who has multiple personality disorder and speaks in rhyme a lot." V handed her a script.

"Excellent," said Sally as if she had nailed it already. Sally always wore dance clothes to school as if life was just a rehearsal for her big break or something. She looked like a runaway extra from the movie *The Turning Point*, waiting in the wings in case Anne Bancroft twisted her ankle and she had to go on.

"Wendy, you will be playing David's mother, Mrs. Clemens, who is domineering, cold, and manipulative." V handed me my copy.

"Thank you, Mr. V," I said. Piece of cake, I thought, I could just pretend to be Mother.

Robin's hand shot up. "What about me?"

"You will be playing the stout Sandra, a sweet girl at the school and friend to Lisa." Mr. V issued Robin a script.

She started leafing through the pages looking for her lines. "What does 'stout' mean?"

"It means 'fat.' Ha!" said Mitch, collapsing onto the floor in guffaws.

"You're a real dick, Mitch," said Robin.

"Now, now. Remember, there are no small parts, just small actors," said V.

"There *are* small parts and that's what I've got," Robin said, sulkily.

V chose to ignore the remark. "Ronnie and Annette will be playing the other kids at the school. Paul is cast as the doctor." V handed out the remaining scripts. "We'll rehearse four days a week after school for four weeks and then perform the play right before Christmas break. That doesn't give us much time; we might have to have a few Saturday rehearsals, but I think this group can pull it off."

There was a silence as we all absorbed the enormity of our task: some of us dreaming of taking our bows to thunderous applause, some worrying about forgetting lines, one troubled by the idea of appearing onstage in a fat suit.

"Get off book as soon as you can. See you at rehearsal."

Robbie and I walked out of V's classroom into the cold fall air and headed for the parking lot.

"You'll get a bigger part in the next show," I said, trying to make her feel better.

"Yeah, maybe." She shrugged as if it didn't matter.

A few days after rehearsals for *David and Lisa* started, Mother, compelled to show that she, too, could be artistic, announced that she was going to start writing a book. It was to be a novel based on her own life, and my sister and I were to be characters in it.

"Of course, when I sell it to the movies, I'll make sure there's a special clause in my contract that says you girls will play yourselves." Mother paced up and down the carpet with visions of limousines double-parked in her head.

"Or how about Jodie Foster? She could play me," I suggested. I didn't want to play myself; I already was playing myself. I'd been acting my pants off as the Dutiful Daughter for a long time and it was hard work.

"Don't you want to be in my movie?" Mother asked, waving her cigarette holder around in the air.

I decided not to say anything.

"I was thinking about who should play me," she went on. "Jane Fonda or Tuesday Weld. I've always really liked Jane, but Tuesday does look more like me."

"Hmmm," I said, frowning to show my appreciation of her casting dilemma. My opinion wasn't really required because Mother wasn't really listening; she was already at the studio commissary having lunch with Tuesday Weld and Richard Zanuck.

"I'm going to call it *Somebody Turn Off the Wind Machine*," she announced with great flourish, striking a theatrical pose worthy of a silent-film heroine.

"Catchy," I said.

I found this image hilarious but utterly in keeping with Mother's warped vision of herself. She was an actress in her own life, a Lillian Gish–type character, playing the part of the brave pioneer woman protecting her children from the harshness of the world, putting out the fire with her gunnysack and raisin' her younguns all alone. Then, at the end of a long day on the set, she could take off her calico dress and her bonnet and retire to her luxurious trailer. There she could enjoy a well-earned cocktail and then get dressed to go out dancing at the Mocambo. This was the mirage she saw herself living in.

Soon she was typing away in the little sunroom off the side of the house. We would go off to school in the morning and there she'd be, with a big cup of coffee next to her humming typewriter, clacking away with her cigarette holder stuck in her teeth. The pile of pages grew higher each day as she compiled her version of the truth.

It was the first real work we had ever seen Mother do. She had never had an actual "job" in the traditional sense, unless you counted trophy wife of a man fifteen years her senior or fabulously neglectful mother of two children. We lived on her alimony check from Pop, and, more recently, money that she had begun to siphon out of our trust accounts from Grandfather. If we needed money—and after she'd blown through her inheritance and sold the Mercedes we always did—she would sit me down and have me call the bank in Kansas City to have them wire a few thousand dollars out of my account. Sometimes I even heard her calling the bank and pretending to be me; she'd make her voice all high and wispy. Mother felt that it was really her money anyway and often reminded us that she expected us to turn it over to her when we inherited it. And apparently now it would enable her to properly furnish the house she'd buy in Beverly Hills when the movie of her book hit the big screen.

In addition to her novel, Mother also announced that she had stopped drinking, sworn off men forever, and was going to therapy sessions once a week at McLean Hospital, conveniently located in our little suburb of Belmont. McLean was a blue-blood nuthouse and drying-out destination. Most of its patients came from families who preferred their names on libraries instead of in newspapers, but it had its celebrity patients, too. Sylvia Plath had gone there for a long rest after a suicide attempt; so had the also famously dead poet Anne Sexton. And it was where Joan Kennedy went for her AA meetings. It catered to a better class of crazy people, and Mother's gyno, Dr. Stander, had somehow convinced her to go. I'm sure the hospital's high-class guest list of the fantastically misunderstood had helped.

It all seemed too good to be true. Which, in a way, was worse for Robin and me. It was like we were waiting for an explosive device to go off.

Rehearsals for *David and Lisa* were going well; we all knew our lines and blocking. Mr. V told us he felt confident we'd be ready on opening night. Robin had agreed to wear a fat suit but had negotiated its removal for curtain call so that people wouldn't think that in real life she was shaped like an oversize beach ball. Mother had consented to let me wear her dark blue suit and high heels, which made me look terrifyingly like her, so much so that I had to be careful not to look in the mirror for fear of scaring myself. We were about two weeks away from the opening when Mr. V asked me to stay after rehearsal. Robin shot me a *You're in for it now* look and went out the big double doors of the auditorium to wait for me.

"Am I in trouble?" I asked him after everyone else had left. I always thought I was in trouble.

"Nothing like that. I thought we should have a little talk about your future."

"Oh," I said, relieved. Sort of.

"Since you're a senior, I was wondering if you'd given any thought to acting as a career." I had but I wasn't sure how to go about it. All my classmates were filling out applications to Yale and Princeton, and it was almost Christmas. I had halfheartedly filled out applications to Colby and Clark, two liberal arts colleges that weren't too far away from home—but I hadn't mailed them in yet. In my experience, the future wasn't something you planned for; it was something that just happened, like your car spinning out on some black ice and hitting a snowbank, or the telephone ringing with bad news in the middle of the night. Mother's plan for my future didn't extend beyond my turning over my trust fund to her and portraying myself in the movie of her life. So I guess you could say that I lacked guidance.

"There's something called the Leagues. It's in January in New York City." V produced a black-and-white brochure from his scuffed-up briefcase. "You can audition for all the big university drama programs at the same time." He handed me the brochure.

"Gee, thanks."

"I would look at Carnegie Mellon, NYU, Northwestern, and Temple. Take it home, look it over, and let me know if you need any help." He sort of coughed, turned, and walked back over to his briefcase.

"Do you think I'm good enough to get into acting school?"

"I do, my talented young friend. But you have to take the

situation by the balls, if you don't mind me saying." He kept shuffling around in his briefcase while he talked rather than looking at me.

"I could take the train down to New York." I wasn't sure the Subaru would make it.

"Yes, you could. If this is what you want to do, you need to be somewhere where you can practice your craft." He shut his briefcase and locked it. Then he looked up at me. "Sound like a plan?"

"Yes, sir. Thank you."

"All right. Good work today." V walked out of the auditorium and I stood there alone for a moment, realizing that the last person who had taken a real interest in me was my English teacher in London, Mr. Jesse. I seemed to be always searching for someone to point me in the right direction, any direction really. And every now and then, someone reached out and took my hand. I put the brochure in my backpack. I had a plan.

Later, during the drive home, Robin asked what V had wanted to talk to me about. I told her that he thought I should apply to acting school.

"Are you going to?" she asked as we drove home in the dark.

"Yeah, I think so."

"Great," she said unenthusiastically, but without a hint of her usual sixteen-year-old snarkiness. We both knew what it meant: I was going to get to escape the Snake Pit and she'd be the one left behind to watch over its sole inmate.

During dinner that night I told Mother that I wanted to apply to acting schools. She sat and listened to me talk about which ones Mr. V thought I should try out for and that he thought that I was good enough to get in. She hardly touched her dinner as I spoke, and then lit up a Dunhill.

"Just remember, Wendy, that acting is all very well and good, but you need to have something to fall back on. I suppose with a college degree you could teach."

"But I don't want to be a teacher. I want to be an actress," I said, looking down into my chicken.

"Well," Mother sighed, "you should at least learn to type so you'll always be able to support yourself. I've known how to type since I was sixteen." Mother had yet to actually use her typing to support herself, or us for that matter, but I wasn't going to point that out.

"Yes, ma'am," I said.

"One hundred and twenty-five words a minute."

"That's a very good idea, Mother. I promise I'll learn how to type."

Robin looked at me mischievously, lips pursed, desperately trying to stifle a smile. I tried to look serious.

My mother stared at me for a beat, then extinguished her cigarette, pushed her chair back, and rose to leave the room, leaving her uneaten dinner on the table.

"Then you'll have a valuable skill, just in case things don't work out," she said over her shoulder as she exited.

Robin started to stack the dishes, scraping the leftovers on top of Mother's full plate. We held our breath until we knew Mother was out of hearing range, then burst out in snorts of laughter.

"Well, Wendy, acting is all very well, but really!" Robin said grandiosely, tossing her hair.

"You need something to fall back on. Just in case!" I giggled, flouncing around self-importantly.

"Yeah, if you can't find some rich guy to take care of you." Robin snatched up a dinner fork from the table and mimed smoking it.

"Some sucker!" I said, laughing even harder.

"I've known how to type since I was nine," Robin oozed. "Four hundred words a minute!" She threw her arm across her forehead and bulged out her eyes, making herself look like Gloria Swanson at the end of *Sunset Boulevard* when they come to take her away to the booby hatch. We both collapsed onto the dining-room chairs in guffaws.

Spent from our big laugh, we wiped our eyes, blew our noses in the cloth napkins, and returned to clearing the table and doing the dishes.

"She is so full of it," Robin said as she washed and I dried.

The next day, we came home from school and there she was, firing away at her typewriter. And next to her on the table was an enormous bouquet of yellow roses. Yellow roses were her favorite.

"Who are those from?" I asked her.

"They're from Frank. Isn't that sweet? He loves me and he wants me back." She didn't look up as she said this but kept typing and smoking. I hadn't seen a box, or any cellophane from the florist, and I asked if he had brought them over himself. But she said no, that he'd had them delivered.

"They're beautiful," I said.

My heart sinking, I went outside into the driveway and looked through the windows of her car. The backseat was littered with yellow rose petals. She had bought the flowers herself and had lied about Frank having sent them. I felt disgusted by how stupid she must think we were, but I also felt sorry for her.

There had been so many bouquets in the old days. The men would always telephone to make sure their flowers were delivered, and I would often have the thrill of asking, "Which ones are yours?" But the flowers had stopped coming long ago. Looking at the rose petals on the backseat of Mother's car, I felt that familiar sense of dread. It was a feeling that something was coming this way. Like a tsunami or a meteorite. And there was nothing I could do to stop it.

I didn't say anything to Robbie about the flowers. Despite my sister's increasing worldliness, I still wished to protect her—playing Pollyanna at any cost. Mother kept up her busy-little-beaver routine, writing in the mornings when we left for school. In the afternoons, she'd still be at it, a full ashtray at her elbow, a chain of lit cigarettes around the house, and a pot of something on the stove. On Thursdays, the day that she went to see her therapist at McLean, she was especially chipper and eager to share some of the details of her therapy session as soon as we got home.

One Thursday after we got home from school, she was bustling around the kitchen chopping vegetables for a stew.

"Hello, girls," she said gaily.

My sister and I exchanged worried looks.

"How was your day?" I asked.

"I'm great. But my doctor thinks that it's because of you girls that I drink." She said this like one would say, did you know that if you throw water on a fire, it goes out? I looked at her. I was stunned that any doctor would say something like that.

The next Thursday at the dinner table she said, "My doctor thinks that if you and your sister appreciated me more, I wouldn't be so depressed." She said it with the same *That's Incredible!* look on her face. My sister and I looked at each other. "Eat your pot roast before it gets cold, girls," she said. I began to wonder what kind of a bozo this shrink was.

A month went by and we performed *David and Lisa* to the usual shock and dismay of the parents. The holidays came and went uneventfully, but the wildly unprofessional remarks from Mother's doctor continued.

The night before her next therapy appointment, I snuck outside and put a rock on the fender of her car. When Robbie and I got home from school the next day, the rock was still there. I did the exact same thing for the next two weeks, and each Thursday after we got home, the rock was on Mother's car fender. On the third Thursday, I pulled into the driveway, saw the rock, and lost it.

"Goddammit!" I exclaimed loudly as I rolled the window down and crawled out of the car. "Goddammit, goddammit." I yanked my backpack out of the backseat, heaved it up onto my shoulder, and headed for the stairs.

"What the hell is wrong with you?" Robin hollered after me.

I marched into the house and there she was, sitting in a cloud of her own smoke in the sunporch.

"How was your therapy session today?" I said sarcastically. I visualized flinging her typewriter through the sunporch window, but I wanted to trip her up in her big fat lie first.

"Oh, fine," she said waving her cigarette around.

"Any life-shattering discoveries?" I sneered.

"Um, no." She shrugged her shoulders.

"What's your doctor's name?" I commanded.

"Epstein." She took a huge drag on her cigarette.

I stomped over to the telephone and picked up the receiver. I called directory assistance and asked for the number of McLean Hospital. Mother watched me calmly, stubbing out a cigarette and then lighting another. I got through to the switchboard, where the operator informed me that there was no doctor named Epstein at the hospital. Then she asked if she could help me with anything. I said no and hung up. I looked at Mother as if to say, *Yes? Well? Is there something you'd like to explain?*

She gave me a frosty look.

Robin walked in. "What's going on?" she demanded, looking back and forth between us.

"I suppose you think you're very clever, Wendy," Mother said archly as she swept by me and up the stairs to her room. *Slam!* went her door a few seconds later.

The Waltons was canceled. Good night, John Boy.

chapter ten

INNER MEDEA

That night, Mother ran out of the house in her nightgown. The sound of her tires on the gravel woke us up, and we dashed out after her just in time to see her peel out of the driveway and reverse into the street. I shouted at her to stop.

"Just let her go," Robin yelled. She grabbed my arm and tried to pull me back toward the dark house. I wrenched away from her, ran to the street, and stood in front of the car, waving my arms in the air. Mother put her foot on the gas, revving the engine theatrically, and headed straight for me.

"Mother! Stop!" I screamed.

I moved a few feet over to the side of the street and she steered toward me. I jumped backward as she approached, throwing myself onto the mounded lawn. Her face was almost unrecognizable over the steering wheel—hair flying, eyes practically screwed shut, and her cigarette glowing from between her bared teeth. She just missed me by sharply turning at the last second, then gunned it down the street. I got up and watched her taillights melt into the blackness. I turned and saw Robin standing in the doorway. We looked at each other with no idea of what to do. It wasn't like there was a manual that tells you what to do when your drunk mom tries to run you over and then drives off at a hundred miles an hour in the middle of the night. It was like a scene in a bad TV movie. Except, of course, it wasn't a movie; it was our life.

We went quickly back into the house and I ran to the sunporch to use the phone to call the police and discovered, in her still-running typewriter, a note announcing her intention to kill herself: Life was no longer worth living, her children hated her, no one loved her, she was ten pounds overweight, and it was time to end it all.

I called the police and gave them a description of the missing person: about five foot four, blue, bloodshot eyes, 110 pounds, wearing a blue nightgown, no shoes, probably drunk, and most likely holding a cigarette.

Robbie stood beside me, arms crossed, tapping her bare foot on the floor.

"Yes, Officer, it's our mother," I said.

"Well, your mother has to be missing for at least twenty-four hours before we can start searching for her," the policeman said.

Robin grabbed the phone away from me. "Look, she left a suicide note! Are you telling me you're not going to do anything?!"

"I'm sorry, but she has to be gone for that amount of time to legally qualify as a missing person."

Of course, we knew she'd been missing for years.

We sat downstairs in the guest bedroom watching a *Columbo* rerun on TV, waiting for her to come back or for a call from the morgue. I prayed for rain to make it easier for her to drive her car off the road. It was going to be a long night.

"I'll go make some popcorn." I went to the kitchen and put a big pot on the stove to heat up the Jolly Time.

"Shit, I have a huge math test tomorrow," Robin said from the other room. "Can you bring me a Tab?"

"Sure," I said, raising my voice over the popping sounds in the pot as I shook it back and forth.

Just as I was grabbing a soda for Robbie out of the fridge, I heard her scream. I ran back into the room and her face was frozen. Wide-eyed, mouth open, she was pointing at the television. I turned to look at the screen and saw a dignified, white-haired man in a suit. He was standing in front of a bookcase, holding up a bottle of vitamins and looking very sincere. There was something about the man that I recognized—he looked familiar but I couldn't think of where I had met him before. I kept staring and he kept talking about the vitamins, then he began to recite a telephone number that appeared at the bottom of the screen. That's when I realized who it was.

It was Daddy.

It was the first time in almost ten years we had seen him

or heard his voice. It was, in fact, the first proof we'd had that he was still alive.

"Oh my God," Robbie gasped.

"His hair's turned white," I whispered.

Although Robbie and I sometimes talked about looking him up, we always decided against it. It was too scary, the fear of rejection too great. Maybe, for once, Mother hadn't lied about his not wanting us. After all, he hadn't tried to find us in all these years. The queer feeling of seeing him on the screen, a stunned shock of recognition, was followed by a flash of anger at the man who had left us to deal with a huge mess. He was most likely peacefully asleep in his bed somewhere, while we were pacing the floor, waiting for the phone to ring from the hospital, or the cops, or a phone booth somewhere. It wasn't fair.

Mother returned from her driving spree two days later, still dressed in the same nightgown and looking bleary. She had a carton of cigarettes tucked under her arm and a crumpled Stop & Shop paper bag, the contents of which I could only guess at.

"Where the hell have you been?" Robbie demanded.

"He's in Europe with his wife." Her voice was flat and dead like her face.

"Who? What are you talking about?" I said.

"Frank. I parked in his driveway and waited for him to come home." Her eyes were all red-rimmed. "Finally the housekeeper came and knocked on my car window."

"You drove to Vermont?" Robbie's disdain was evident, but Mother was too zonked to notice.

Mother continued, ignoring us. "She said he was away skiing somewhere with his wife."

Robbie shook her head and looked at the ceiling.

Mother started to move past me leadenly, making a break for the stairs and her room. "In fucking Europe. I'm living in a rental the size of a shoebox and that bastard is off in a ski lodge in the Alps drinking hot buttered rum."

"We called the police! We had no idea where you were!" Robbie spat furiously.

"I ran out of cigarettes so I decided to come home." With that Mother heaved a sigh, emitting dangerous levels of nicotine that caused my eyes to water as she climbed the stairs, returning to the only place where she seemed to feel safe.

A few days later, I gathered my courage and knocked on her bedroom door. Things had spiraled so out of control, I decided I needed to talk to someone about it other than myself.

Her television was on full blast so I had to shout. "Mother? Mother, are you in there?" Of course I knew she was. "I need to ask you a question!" I listened at the door for some sound.

"In Japan, the hand can be used like a knife!" boomed the announcer on the TV.

I knocked again, this time a little harder. "It's important!"

"Not even this tin can can dull a Ginsu!"

I put my mouth up to the crack in the doorway and said, "I was thinking that I'd like to go to a therapist."

Suddenly I heard the key in the lock and the door opened. She was still in her nightgown, which had not been laundered since her excursion to Vermont. She had stopped frosting her hair again, and it had grown out so that the top of her head was a mop of dishwater blond from which hung a fringe of lighter hair, giving her the overall appearance of a deranged capuchin monkey. Her room smelled like an overflowing ashtray. I glanced over her shoulder to see that she had written in black ink all over her bedsheets what looked like names and phone numbers that I couldn't make out. Empty cans and ice cream cartons were on the floor. It looked like a rock band had gone berserk.

"Therapist?" She looked at me quizzically, twirling her cigarette as if it were her extra finger. "What do you want to talk to a therapist about?"

"Oh, just stuff," I stammered.

"Not me, I hope." She said this to me as if I were accusing her of borrowing my favorite sweater.

"Oh, no, not you. Me."

"You?" She looked confused. I could see that it was mind-boggling to Mother that I might think of myself as a worthy and interesting topic of discussion.

"Yes, just me and school and, you know, being a teenager."

She considered this for a moment, then shrugged her shoulders. "Well, all right, what the hell, go ahead. But remember, therapy can be a crutch."

"Yes, Mother." I decided not to mention her foray into pretend therapy.

She shut the door and turned the TV up louder.

Dr. Keylor's office was in her house in a suburb of Boston not far from my school. She had a friendly, round face, brown hair, and wore chunky jewelry. She looked like someone's mom—not mine, but someone's.

"Can you tell me something about why you are here?" she asked in her calm, reassuring voice. I started to tell her and noticed her eyes getting wider and wider as I kept talking. She scribbled on a yellow legal pad, handed me the Kleenex box, and at the end of the hour told me she wanted to see me twice a week.

At my next session, after I had regaled Dr. Keylor with the story of Thanksgiving in the ER and the events following, she told me that my mother was "psychotic," a nifty word I had never heard before.

"You mean, like, crazy?" I asked.

"Therapists dislike the word *crazy*," she answered slowly. "Let's just say that your mother is mentally deranged and has lost contact with external reality."

The following week, Dr. Keylor showed me a page in a huge book—the *Diagnostic and Statistical Manual of Mental Disorders*.

"I want you to take a few minutes and read about these particular personality disorders." She ran her finger along the words *narcissistic* and *histrionic*. "I believe your mother suffers from both of these psychological conditions, and we call this diagnosis a Cluster B."

I thought *Cluster B* sounded like an elaborate math problem or a healthy candy bar. I pored over the list of symptoms, which included lack of empathy, excessive emotionality, inappropriate seductiveness, and needing constant admiration. I felt that my mother's picture should have been right there on the page.

"This is incredible, Dr. Keylor. Thanks for showing it to me."

"Of course, Wendy. I'll see you on Monday at three thirty. Have a nice weekend." She wrote my appointment time on a card and handed it to me.

Armed with all this new information, I felt enormously relieved. It wasn't my imagination that my home life was frighteningly bizarre. Now I had the validation of a health-care professional. I felt as if I had made an amazing discovery—one that I could share only with Robbie.

The truth was I was ashamed and embarrassed by my mother and would have done anything to conceal what went on in my home. My secret was safe with Dr. Keylor, and my mother could occasionally pull it together and make a public appearance. She'd put on her Chanel suit and her pearls, do her hair and makeup, and come see the school play with her mink around her shoulders. Afterward, she would chat with the other parents and annoy the hell out of the headmaster by smoking in the auditorium. The kids would marvel at how glamorous she looked. My friend Nancy Higgins gushed, "Wow, your mom is so cool. She looks like a movie star!" I wanted to tell Nancy that I hated my mother, that she was a crazy bitch, and that if Nancy knew what she was really like, she would hate her just as much as I did. But instead I smiled and said, "Thanks."

I had another secret, one that I planned to keep from Mother for as long as possible. I had a boyfriend. His name was Dylan. He was in my class and had longish blond hair, wore glasses, and played the guitar. We didn't travel in the same circles; he was one of the "cool" stoner kids, but he got all A's in school. I had first noticed him when he performed the Elvis Costello song "Alison" in the Beaver Talent Show. His voice was thin and cracked in places during the song, but something about him up onstage playing the guitar with his eyes shut and his head thrown back got to me in a way nothing ever had before. He rocked along as he played, spastically dancing in a mustard-colored suit that he wore with a skinny black tie. He looked goofy and exposed and I felt like he was singing to me.

"'Alison, I know this world is killing you. Oh, Alison, my aim is true.'"

He didn't win the contest; Phillippa Freiberg won for her baton-twirling routine done to the *Star Wars* theme.

The only other boy at Beaver who I'd had a crush on was a hunky lacrosse player named Kirk Winthrop, a golden boy who barely acknowledged my presence. Having no idea how to get him to notice me, I had decided to ignore him, thinking that my icy stare off into the distance would drive him wild. So far, it hadn't worked. I decided to take a different tack with Dylan. After he lost, I went right up to him in the auditorium and I told him that I thought he should have won, not that lame cheerleader girl.

"That's wicked nice of you," he said. His teeth were a little crooked and he was a tad cross-eyed, which made him look so sweet, like a little boy.

Soon we were eating lunch together in the school cafeteria and I was going over to his house on weekends. His parents were both professors and totally relaxed about everything. They smoked pot and walked around the house practically naked in these big kimonos that hung open. When I went to Dylan's house we were allowed to go into his room and shut the door for hours, and his parents not only didn't mind, they hardly seemed to notice. They had a free and easy way; they weren't drunk all the time, just stoned sometimes, and they never screamed or threw things.

I had kissed a few boys in London and had even slapped one on the face for sticking his tongue in my mouth, which I thought, at the time, was very uncouth. And then there were stage kisses in the school play. That was where you pressed your dry, closed lips together and waited about five to ten seconds (depending how in love you were in the play), and the only thing you'd feel was embarrassment and the air from the other person's nostrils on your face as the person breathed through them. But making out with Dylan was different.

One Saturday afternoon we were in his room making

out when he pushed my head down to his crotch. I had no idea what he was doing. He just kept steering me down toward his zipper.

"What are you doing?" I knew nothing about sex and was probably the last virgin standing in my class.

"I want you to put it in your mouth." He wiggled his eyebrows up and down in a naughty way. This was the weirdest thing I'd ever heard. I just couldn't believe that anyone would do that.

"You're kidding, right?" I smiled and tossed my hair back, trying desperately to look as if I weren't terrified by the thought of seeing his penis that close up—or at all, actually. Trying to be cool, I told him I'd touch it but I wouldn't put it in my mouth.

"Please," he begged, pushing my head even harder down south.

I thought about how much I loved him, how we belonged together, how we were the same person.

"Pleeeease, Wendy."

I wanted to make him happy so I screwed my eyes shut and felt around for his zipper, pretending to be a blind girl in a French art movie. It wasn't so bad except for the end part, which tasted like that gross baking-soda toothpaste that I had tried once before throwing away the tube.

Sometimes I did it for so long, my jaw felt like it was going to fall off. To keep my mind off how uncomfortable it was, I thought about other stuff, such as homework, or all my old school-locker combinations, or naming the six wives of Henry VIII in order. I tried to come up with something he could do to me that would make me feel as good as I made him feel. But I couldn't think of anything.

It was important to hide the fact that I had a boyfriend from Mother for as long as I could. I had learned this lesson the year before when Tommy Manucci started mowing our lawn. Tommy Manucci was eighteen, had thick, curly, black hair, and was gorgeous. He also didn't know I was alive. On Mondays, after I finished my homework, I would lower the shade in my room and crouch down to look at him through the bottom of the window so that he couldn't see me staring at him. He usually took his shirt off about halfway through his work, which was my favorite part. I just loved to watch him mow our lawn. I gazed at his sweaty chest and the hair stuck to his forehead, and the smell of the cut grass would fill my room. I closed my eyes and, inhaling deeply, I imagined us rolling in that grass, it getting stuck on our bodies and tangled in our hair as we rolled down the hill locked in an ardent embrace. He was the first boy I had a physical ache for. Being a late bloomer, I had never experienced these feelings before and made the mistake of talking to my mother about them.

"You know, Wendy, boys that age are already having sex." She eyed me suspiciously. Sixteen and tragically nerdy, I certainly was not.

"I just think he's handsome." Feeling all hot and prickly,

I suddenly realized how stupid I had been to confide in her. Most girls could talk to their mothers and not have it be ammunition that could be used against them later. But not me.

"A boy that age is only interested in one thing."

"All I said was that . . ." I had foolishly lowered my guard and tried now to backpedal.

"You've grown up without a father." Mother shook her head as if it were my fault. "I don't want you to confuse sex with love."

"I'm not going to have sex with him, I just think he's cute." I pedaled faster.

"And he's *Italian*."

"So?" I didn't get the connection.

"Very hot-blooded. God knows what could happen."

She made him sound like a rapist. I was sure that once he noticed I was alive, he would never pressure me into anything I wasn't ready for.

"You stay away from him, young lady."

"Yes, ma'am."

It turned out I didn't have to worry about his raping me because a couple of Mondays later, after I watched him mow the lawn, I heard my mother call to him. He turned off the lawn mower and started to put his shirt back on. Mother walked up to him and was talking to him, but I couldn't hear what she was saying. I noticed that she was wearing a halter top. I didn't even know she owned a halter top. My heart started to beat so fast that it hurt. I watched in horror as Mother reached out to him and put her hand on his arm. Then she started to steer him in the direction of the little pup tent in our yard that Robbie and I had been planning to spend the night in as soon as it got warmer. Experiencing chest pain, I ran to the guest-room window so I could see where they were heading. I saw my mother take Tommy into the tent. I sat down on the bed. She apparently had come up with an alternative form of payment. They emerged about twenty minutes later. Mother was smiling and chewing on a piece of grass. The boy who cut our grass got into his truck and drove away. Mother waved. He never came back.

"No, Wendy, seducing the lawn boy is not normal behavior." Dr. Keylor shook her head with an air of distaste.

I explained to Dr. Keylor that I was not eager to introduce Mother to Dylan. She didn't need to meet him anyway because soon he and I would be living in some fabulous city far away where I would pursue my acting career and he would be playing guitar in a rock band. Dr. Keylor assured me that my dream of getting away and living my own life wasn't just an idle fantasy; it might not work out exactly the way I wanted it to, but I was taking steps in the right direction.

"Good luck in New York," Dr. Keylor said with a smile and a little squeeze of my arm.

That weekend I took the train down to New York, where the auditions for the Leagues were being held at the Warwick Hotel on Sixth Avenue and Fifty-fourth Street. It was a freezing cold day, but I walked the blocks around the hotel trying to calm my nerves. There were memories for me all along those sidewalks. There were the smelly horse carriages outside the Plaza, where Robbie and I had once ridden through the park with Mother and a man she had picked up at the Oak Bar with a bottle of pilfered champagne. There was the GM Building, where the Auto Pub used to be. Robin and I loved to go there because you ate inside a car and watched a movie that was projected up on the wall. I passed FAO Schwarz, where we had once ridden a slide that went from the second floor down to the first. The city seemed different now, louder and dirtier and filled with more people. Putting the New York of my childhood behind me, I circled back to the Warwick.

I was sitting on the floor outside one of the hotel ballrooms where they were holding the auditions in my leotard and wraparound skirt. I was trying not to feel too horribly nervous when a pair of fashionable black pumps with little bows on them stopped in front of me.

"Excuse me, dear, are you Wendy Rea?" I was just reading the word *Ferragamo* on the shoes when I looked up and saw a petite, elegantly dressed woman with coiffed silver hair.

"Yes, I am."

"I'm Betty Rea, dear. I saw your name on the list and I thought I'd come over and wish you good luck." This was my stepfather's first wife; the woman whom my stepfather had deserted for Mother. My mother had ruined her life, and she was wishing me good luck on my audition.

I thought it was very classy of her. I got up off the floor and thanked her.

"You look just the same, dear. Just like your father. How is he?"

"Oh, fine," I lied. She told me that if I moved to New York, I must call her; she was the head of casting at a soap opera and she would give me some extra work.

"Very good experience, you know, to be in front of the camera." She handed me her card.

"Thank you, that's very kind of you." We shook hands.

"Break a leg, dear." She gave me a cheerful wave over her shoulder as she walked away. I thanked her again and she was gone.

"Next, we'd like to see Wendy Rea."

I went in and performed my monologues in front of a table filled with silent onlookers. No one said anything, and most of the people didn't even look at me; they were hunched over, writing on pads of paper. One man ate a whole pie during my audition. The entire experience was completely unnerving. I came out with no impression of how I had done.

I took the train back to Boston that evening. Mother picked me up at South Station in her nightgown and immediately started talking about how painful life was. I was exhausted and not really listening at first, not interested in her philosophical musings. I did notice that she hadn't asked me about the tryout, but I was too tired to tell her about it and I certainly wasn't going to mention seeing the first Mrs. Oliver Rea.

"You know, I've been thinking very hard about this terrible pain that is life." She sounded like Greer Garson in *Mrs. Miniver*—very noble and all that.

I looked out the window at the dark streets of Boston. I just wanted to go to bed.

"I've begun to think that the best thing for me to do is to kill you and your sister and then myself," she continued in a calm voice. "That is the only way you won't have to go through what I've been through. If you and your sister were dead, you wouldn't have to suffer, to feel this pain."

Great, I thought, *I probably just bombed out of drama school and now my mom wants to kill me.* I put my hand on the door handle so I could jump out of the car if she decided to crash it into a tree.

"You just don't know how much agony I would be sparing you. It's so hard." She pulled into the driveway and turned off the engine, then looked at me and said in a perfectly matter-of-fact way, "You see, Wendy, the truth is, life isn't worth living." Then she smiled.

I got out of the car and went upstairs to my sister's room. She was sound asleep. I closed the door and propped a chair beneath the door handle. Then I crawled into bed next to her and spent the night listening to every creak and ping, expecting Mother tiptoeing upstairs with a kitchen knife, channeling her inner Medea.

chapter eleven

SMOKE AND MIRRORS

After returning from New York and my first assault on the world of the theater, I prepared myself for the next big event in my life: having sex for the first time with Dylan. I drove to the Planned Parenthood clinic in Cambridge to secure the necessary equipment.

I sat up on the examination table in a paper dress waiting for the doctor to come in. I had left my socks on because I was cold. I stared at the brightly colored oven mitts with a kitty cat pattern on them that covered the stirrups at the opposite end of the table. I wondered if the oven mitts were meant to keep the stirrups warm or to help catch a flying baby. On one wall was a large medical drawing of the female reproductive system with everything labeled in large red letters, as if issuing a warning: DANGER—UTERUS AHEAD! On the other wall was a travel poster advertising the Swiss Alps. I pondered the possible connection between the vagina and all that snow and ice. Would losing my virginity be exciting, like being transported to the top of the highest mountain, or would I be frigid, feel nothing, and wish I'd stayed home? There were no magazines to look at in the room, so I bit my fingernails while I worried and waited.

There was a knock on the door, and in walked a very tall, dignified-looking woman. She was wearing a black velvet hair band to keep her bobbed gray hair back, and she had on tasteful pearl earrings. She wore a tweed skirt and a light blue cashmere sweater underneath her white coat. She looked like my English teacher, Miss Thompson, who gave me good grades on my creative-writing assignments and asked me to read from Shakespeare in class. Looking at her, I suddenly felt out of danger. She glanced down at a clipboard that had my medical form on it.

"Wendy? I'm Dr. Mayher." She looked at me with a bright smile. I nodded and smiled back. "I just have a few questions I need to ask you before we start the examination." I nodded again. "Are you sexually active?"

"Um, no, but I hope to be." I noticed that the kittens on the stirrup pot holders were playing with little balls of yarn.

"So you've never had any sexually transmitted diseases." She wrote on my chart, sounding slightly disappointed.

"Well, I had a yeast infection once. Does that count?" I wanted Dr. Mayher to like me. Jesus, I was so pathetic.

"No, dear, not the same thing." Then she asked me how old I was.

"Seventeen." Then, just so she didn't think I was a slut, I added, "But I'll be eighteen in a few months."

"All right." She finished writing on my chart. "Now, why don't you lie down and try to relax."

I took a deep breath and placed my feet in the cheerful oven mitts.

"This will feel very cold."

I turned my head and gazed again at the poster of the Alps, clasping my hands together on my chest like a nun. I flinched slightly at the icy feel of the speculum going inside me and tried to think tranquil thoughts: raindrops on roses and whiskers on kittens, bright copper kettles and warm woolen mittens. For the next few minutes it felt as if Dr. Mayher were rearranging my internal organs the way you move furniture around in a room—rolling up the rug, lifting the coffee table, and pushing the sofa against the wall—but it was inside me. Then it was over. I felt the speculum come out and heard it clatter onto a tray.

"Everything looks fine, dear, you can sit up. Now we have to discuss your options. The easiest is really the pill."

I explained to Dr. Mayher that I didn't want to take the pill because my friends had told me it made you fat and made your skin break out.

Dr. Mayher laughed. "Well, we can just fit you for a diaphragm, dear." She started poking around in a different drawer. "Not to worry."

Twenty minutes later, I left the clinic with a diaphragm in its own little pink case and an industrial-size tube of

Ortho-Gynol stashed in my backpack. I hurried home to practice.

Checking to make sure that Mother was barricaded in her room, I headed for the bathroom and locked the door. I pulled down my pants and opened the pink case. I put the spermicidal jelly inside the diaphragm and around the rim and folded it so it looked like a rubber mini-taco.

"What are you doing in there?" Robin shouted from the hall as she turned the doorknob.

"Nothing!" I almost dropped the diaphragm into the toilet.

"Well, I have to pee!"

I managed to insert the diaphragm, but I had used too much killer jelly and my hands were covered in it. "I'm going as fast as I can!" I didn't want to wipe it on the hand towel, so I hobbled over to the sink with my pants around my ankles.

"Hurry!"

I washed my hands and at the same time I used my foot to flush the toilet to create a diversion. "Just give me a minute." I stuffed my contraception items into my backpack. The hefty tube of Ortho-Gynol was especially unwieldy and really unsexy. I was going to have to shop for a non-jumbo size that could fit in my purse. If Dylan saw me whip this big sucker out, I'd stay a virgin.

When I opened the door, Robbie eyed me weirdly. "What the hell is going on in there?" She looked around behind me like she was hoping to catch me with some guy.

"Nothing, nothing. I just really had to, you know . . . um, you know, go." I fastened my jeans, trying to look nonchalant.

"You've been in here for an hour. Get outta my way."

"I have not. Jeez, relax."

"You relax, my bladder is gonna blow up." She pushed past me.

"I was hoping you could run lines with me," I called after her.

Our last Drama Club production of the year was to be Friedrich Dürrenmatt's black comedy *The Visit*. I was playing the lead, Claire Zachanassian, a grotesque and much-married millionairess who travels back to her hometown to confront the man who ruined her life years before when he impregnated and abandoned her, forcing her into prostitution. Now on her sixth husband, rich and with a wooden leg and a hand carved out of ivory, Claire buys up the entire town and, at the end of the play, bribes the villagers to murder her old lover. It wasn't exactly *Guys and Dolls*, and we were all psyched about the shock value for the Beaver parents on opening night.

"Sure, meet me in my room," Robbie answered.

We ran lines sitting on her bed. Her room was larger than mine and got more light during the day. An inexpensive stereo, the kind with the plastic lid, was on a low table at the end of her bed. Robbie liked to listen to the Doors and Bob Seger. The curtains matched the bedspread and had an oriental flower pattern in navy blue and orange. It was very much the bedroom of an American teenager, except for the little shelf with the broken remains of her precious music-box collection, which were laid out like strange and delicate bones in some macabre children's museum.

"You want to know a secret?" I asked, closing my script and lowering my voice.

"Sure." She scooched over next to me on the bed.

"Well, I think Dylan and I are going to you know what." I was hoping I wouldn't have to go into more detail than that.

"Omigod!" She covered her mouth with both her hands. "When?"

"Soon." I didn't want to tell her that I was shooting for the weekend.

"But how do you know? Did he ask you to? Did you ask him?"

"No, nothing like that. I just know. I know he's the one and that he feels the same way about me."

"Wow." She flopped back onto the bed and looked at the ceiling. "Janice Ruzika told me that you look different after you do it."

"Really?" Did that mean other people would know just by looking at me? "I feel like we belong to each other; that this was meant to be," I said dreamily.

"That's weird. I don't get it." She looked at me like I was bonkers.

"When you fall in love, you'll see what I mean."

"Well, I've already decided that I'm never doing it." She shook her head and looked as if she had a bad taste in her mouth.

"But you might want to one day."

"No way. Boys are buttheads."

I looked at her and smiled. She was still a young girl, my baby sister. I was so much more mature and worldly. She couldn't understand how profound the connection between Dylan and me was. Our physical union would be so beautiful and life changing.

Eight days after my eighteenth birthday, Dylan and I went back to his house after school and raced up the stairs to his bedroom. He drew the curtains, and the only light was the glow from his fish tank, which threw a bluish hue across the floor. We lay down on the rug beside his bed and looked into each other's eyes.

"I love you," he said. He took off his glasses and tossed them over his shoulder onto his single bed, looking at me like some super-suave guy who'd done this a million times. All I felt was scared and nervous. Desperately trying to hide it, I took off my wristwatch and threw it on the bed in the same nonchalant way. He laughed, then kissed me while he unbuttoned my shirt.

"I love you, too," I whispered into his hair. I struggled out of my cords until I was just in my bra and underwear. Dylan was already naked. I felt as if everyone I'd ever known could see me and was watching what I was doing, even though just the two of us were in the dark room. My face felt all red and hot and I wondered if I should apologize for the size of my breasts. I sat up and unhooked my bra. Dylan pulled off my panties and lifted himself on top of me. I looked up at his face hovering above mine, searching his eyes for some clue or hint as to what to do. I didn't see one, so I closed my eyes.

Then he covered me with his body and I could feel him pushing into me. It hurt at first but then it stopped. He started to move faster and I placed my hands on his shoulders as if to keep him from flying away, then he sort of collapsed on top of me and didn't move. I opened my eyes and looked up at the little fish darting around in the tank flashing yellow, green, and blue.

"Are you okay?" I asked. Was it over? Was he dead? I placed my hands flat on his back and felt his slow, deep breathing.

"Yeah." He rolled off me onto the floor. "Wow, Wendy, that was great."

I wanted to ask what was so great about it, but I didn't. I smiled weakly at him and thought that I shouldn't have been in such a big hurry to do it and could have waited, say, another ten years or so. Dylan picked up his guitar and strummed it, broadly grinning. For a second I hated him. He looked so pleased with himself for taking something from me that I could never get back. It wasn't fair that I didn't feel as good as he did. *Oh, well,* I thought. *Maybe it will be better next time.* At least one of us was happy.

In my next session with Dr. Keylor, I spilled the beans that I was no longer a virgin.

"I see." She scribbled on her pad. Her big, carved wooden bracelets clacked. "And are you using birth control?"

I told her about going to the clinic.

"Good. And how did it make you feel?" In anticipation, she handed me the Kleenex box.

"Kind of lonely. Mad." I proceeded to leak.

"That's all very normal, Wendy. There are many confusing emotions that accompany a first sexual experience."

Then Dr. Keylor asked me about my father. I told her about the last time I had seen him, the Christmas I was eleven and Mother had played reverse Santa Claus, confiscating our toys.

"I'm afraid we have to stop, Wendy." I looked up at the clock; we were ten minutes over. Dr. Keylor had a pained look on her face as she put down her legal pad, took off her glasses, and rubbed her eyes. "I'm sorry . . . I have another patient waiting."

I glanced at the photos on her desk of a teenage boy and girl around the same age as me and wondered what her kids were like. They both had dark hair like her and brown eyes. In one of the photos they were standing on the beach with fishing poles. The boy was smiling, showing his braces, and the girl was looking down shyly at the ground. They looked healthy and preppy, like children in an L.L. Bean catalog.

"Thanks, Dr. Keylor."

"Of course, dear. I'll see you next week. Oh, and Wendy," she said as she walked me to the door, "if you need to talk to me, if there's some kind of problem or emergency before our next session . . ." She stopped and looked at me with a worried expression.

"Yes?"

She jotted down something on the back of the appointment card she always handed me at the end of our time together. "This is my home phone number. You can leave a message here after office hours, but you can also call me at home. If you need to."

I took the card, thanked her, and said good-bye. I drove home wondering if my father ever thought about me. Did he wonder what I looked like? What color my hair was and what was my favorite food? What was he doing right now?

I was grateful to Dr. Keylor for the safe haven, where I could deposit the goings-on past and present of the Snake Pit. She had even offered to float my therapy bill, allowing me to pay it off when I was able to, at some point in the future.

When I pulled up in front of our house, I could see Robin's bedroom light on and the flickering yellow glow behind the shade in Mother's room from the television. I trudged up to the front door, feeling wrung out. All this spilling-my-guts stuff made me want to go to sleep for a year.

The following weekend, on a sunny Saturday, I got an idea of how I'd done at my League audition when I opened rejection letters from all of the schools I'd applied to: Carnegie Mellon, Juilliard, Temple, and NYU had all passed on the chance to groom me for stardom. Mother had been right when she had told me I should have something to fall back on. Clearly, I couldn't cut it. I was devastated.

I ran upstairs, threw myself onto my bed, and buried my face in my pillow to sob away the disappointment.

Robbie came in and sat beside me. She placed her hand on my back, moving it back and forth. "I'm really sorry. I know you must be super bummed out."

I couldn't raise my head to speak. I just nodded into my pillow and kept crying.

"I brought you a glass of water," she whispered. When we were little, the one who was not crying would go get the one who was a drink of water. It made you feel better.

"Thanks." I sat up, sniffling.

"You can try again next year," Robbie said, smiling at me like it was all going to be okay.

After I was sufficiently recovered, she drove us in the Subaru, in her Mario Andretti style, to Bailey's, an old-fashioned marble-tabled place in Harvard Square, where we gorged on coffee ice cream cones, slathered in jimmies. Then we walked to Nini's Corner, the newsstand up the block, and bought a box of Sobranie Cocktail cigarettes, which were hot-pink- and pistachio-colored in a shiny black-and-gold box. We strode smoking them through Harvard Yard arm in arm, speaking in Russian accents, pretending to be kick-ass Bond girls. We had survived all the helter-skelter times and still had each other—our sisterhood, the only thing we could count on.

The one school I hadn't heard from was Boston University. I had applied to the school of liberal arts as a backup, but now it was my only chance. Word of my bombing out spread

quickly through the entire school. Since Beaver was supposedly a "college preparatory school," it would look bad if
I didn't get in anywhere. Paying that stiff Beaver tuition was
supposed to be a guarantee of entrance into a fine university.
A flurry of faculty meetings took place, and Mr. Valentine
kindly volunteered to call BU and "secure" me a spot for the
fall term. He kept me after class that week and told me he
had contacts there and that I was not to worry. BU was a
stone's throw from my house, so not only were my dreams of
a life in the theater dashed, so was my plan to escape. V tried
to make me feel better by telling me that I could probably
reapply next year and transfer into the university's school for
the arts. He was being so nice, but I still felt like a loser.

Dylan was my anchor at school, walking down the hallways with his arm around me while the other kids avoided
making eye contact with me. I was the embarrassment of
Beaver Country Day—the kid who didn't get in anywhere,
and they were all going to Harvard or Cornell.

"Fuck them, man," Dylan said to me as he leaned over
the lunch table in the cafeteria and looked meaningfully into
my eyes. "They're all just robots, doing what their parents
want them to do anyway." He told me he was glad I wasn't
going away to school, because he'd be staying in Boston to
attend the Berklee College of Music. This way we could still
be together. Dylan was the only thing in my life going right.

The next morning, Mother came wafting into my room.
She had been on hiatus from writing the Great American
Novel and was back in her blue-nightgown period. She

slowly walked around my room, filling it with smoke from her Merit, perhaps hoping to find drug paraphernalia or a beer can or two. She stopped beside me and saw the photo of Dylan I had taped to the full-length mirror on the inside of my closet door.

"And who, may I ask, is this?"

Since I was now eighteen, I didn't see any point in lying. "That's my boyfriend, Mother."

"I see. Does he have a name?" She stood close and peered at his face.

"It's Dylan. Dylan Sweeney."

"And have you had sex with him?" She continued to stare at Dylan's face.

This is it, I thought. Forgetting, once again, that telling the truth had always got me in trouble, I told her, "Yes. You don't have to worry, though. I mean, we're using birth control."

She turned and looked at me, tilting her head and smiling like a demented Mrs. Olson in the Folgers coffee commercial.

"My baby," she muttered softly, then bobbed from the room, all glassy eyed. I heard her door shut, followed by loud sobbing.

I didn't know if Mother's crying was genuine or an act, if she was mourning my virginity, or if she was disappointed she hadn't got to my boyfriend first.

The following day, Dylan met me at my locker with his books. "Hey, your mom invited me to lunch at your house on Sunday." He was smiling.

My heart sank. "Really?" Clearly he didn't know that this was probably the worst news I'd received since not getting into theater school.

"Yeah, she called and talked to my mom. Cool, huh?"

I pulled my science book out of my locker and tried not to throw up on it. "You aren't going to come, are you?" I laughed nervously and fidgeted around in my purse for a pencil. I resisted the urge to get into my locker and shut the door.

"Well, of course I am! She invited me." He shook his head and looked at me like I was nuts.

"Dylan, there's something I have to tell you." How could I explain to him that if he came, he'd be walking into the abyss, the Bermuda Triangle, the Cave of the She Bear.

"What? I think it's awesome." Although Dylan was supersmart and got A's in everything, he was not complicated. I think that this sweetness and naïveté were my favorite things about him. He just didn't see all the badness and evil in the world that I knew was out there. How could I get him to understand?

"My mother is not . . . she's not . . ." I struggled to find a word that would both help him grasp the situation and frighten him enough to keep him away. "She's strange. And weird. Really weird. She's not like other mothers."

"Okay. So? No big deal."

I tried again. "She has a dark side. And it's, well, very dark. Very."

"Jeez, Wendy, she's just your mom, not friggin' Darth Vader."

I wanted to grab him and shake him and say, *But she is Darth Vader!* Instead I smiled and, feeling queasy, headed down the hall with him to our first class.

Dylan came to lunch at our house the following Sunday. Mother was on her best behavior when she wanted to impress someone, especially a man. I, of course, was immune to her charms. I watched as she sat a little too close to Dylan on the sofa, showing him pictures in a photo album of me when I was younger.

"Here's Wendy on her second birthday blowing out the candles on her cake. She was a beautiful baby, don't you think?"

Mother had got her hair done and put on a low-cut, ivory crepe-de-chine blouse and black trousers. She was really piling it on, and I could tell Dylan was uncomfortable. He simply wasn't accustomed to a woman his mother's age treating him like her gentleman caller. She'd narrow her eyes, slightly lean in toward him, and part her lips before she spoke. He shot me a few looks of slight panic when she wasn't fixing her languid gaze upon him.

"Here we are in Amsterdam. She's thirteen or so. Isn't that a nice outfit she's wearing? We stopped there after a summer cruise down the Rhine."

Dylan nodded and smiled at her, pointing to someone in the photo. "So who's this? Is this Wendy's dad?"

"Heavens, no. We were divorced ages ago. That was my boyfriend at the time, Giuseppe."

"He's a good-looking guy, Mrs. Rea."

"Yes, he was very handsome. He spoke no English, I spoke no Italian, so he would speak to me in Spanish and I would answer in French." Mother laughed coyly like a debutante and played with her pearls.

Giuseppe had been Mother's boyfriend during a break in her on-again, off-again affair with Pop. They had met on the boat, and soon he was traveling with us. He was Marcello Mastroianni gorgeous and five or six years younger than my mother, and at fourteen I found it all kind of confusing. I instantly developed a terrible crush on him and, for the first and only time ever, found myself wishing I was my mother so that Giuseppe would look at me the way he looked at her. But he didn't because I was his girlfriend's daughter and just a kid. He was great with Robbie and me. One thing my sister and I hated was some guy who thought that because he was with our mother he had to try to be our dad and exert some sort of influence over us. Giuseppe just wanted to take us out to lunch and buy us things, so we were crazy about him, me especially.

On our final day in Amsterdam, we walked down a cobblestone street to a square filled with young, scruffy people playing guitars and sitting around on the ground. Some of them were smoking joints. Suddenly, we heard a siren, and two VW buses drove up onto the pavement. Police armed with clubs started pouring out of the buses and beating the hippies with their sticks. People were screaming and running, trying to get away. We were right in the middle of the square and had no way to escape without passing through the police battle. Giuseppe pushed us all onto the sidewalk and threw his body over us, shielding us from the riot. I could hear screams and shouts, then I heard the doors of the VW buses slam closed, followed by silence. For a long time I remembered that day, lying on the sidewalk with Giuseppe's body shielding us—the way his cologne smelled, the sheen of his hair, and his eyes covered by sunglasses just like a character in a Fellini movie. My Marcello.

"Thanks for inviting me, Mrs. Rea. It was nice to meet you. I enjoyed myself very much." Dylan stuck out his hand to Mother and she took it, enveloping it with her slender fingers like a spider.

"You're very welcome, Dylan. Good-bye."

I walked him outside to his car.

"Jesus." He smiled in that goofy way he had. "I couldn't tell if I was there to see you or to see your mom."

"You were perfect. I can tell she really likes you." Of course, this wasn't much of a compliment. Mother liked anything in pants. I kissed him and looked up into his slightly crossed eyes.

"Well, I'm glad I passed, I guess."

I knew this time it wouldn't be like Tommy Manucci the lawn-mower boy. It would be different because Dylan loved me; he wanted me. She couldn't take him away. I didn't have to worry.

And I didn't worry the whole next week. Dylan and I

held hands and kissed on the soccer field. I went over to his house after school and we did it in his room. He played his guitar and called me "babe." We talked about how we'd see each other all the time because I would be at BU and he was going to Berklee, just a few blocks away. It was almost as if the dream might come true.

Then Mother started calling his house. Sometimes she'd call ten times a day. If she was drunk, she'd shout obscenities into the phone. If she was sober, she'd demand to know if his parents knew we were sleeping together. His parents took it in stride, as if my mother were an annoying telemarketer, but it freaked Dylan out. He began being stone-faced and silent with me. He started making excuses not to see me and went back to hanging out with the cool kids at school who cut class and smoked pot—a group I was not part of.

At Patty Golden's end-of-the-year party, he didn't even show up. At Kenny Pratt's party, he ignored me. I felt sick to my stomach as I watched him stand as far away from me as he could. He was laughing and holding a big, red plastic cup. I had heard that the boys had a keg hidden in the bushes. I wanted to walk over to him, grab the cup from his hand, and toss it in his face to wipe that nice-guy smile off it, while screaming, *You coward! You don't even have the guts to stand up to a crazy woman. And I even told you she was crazy!* But I didn't have the courage to go over to him. I went out on the dance floor and danced by myself. I closed my eyes and moved around to the Earth, Wind & Fire song that was playing:

"Hearts of fire . . . take you high and higher to the world you belong."

I twirled around and wished some giant hand would sweep down and pluck me up and away from all this horrid emptiness I was feeling. Even though he had been ignoring me for weeks, I still loved him. I just didn't know any better.

Dylan officially broke up with me a week later, right before graduation. He had asked me to meet him at the scruffy little park near his house. It was doomsday hot; the trees were curling in the sun. We sat on concrete benches next to the dead grass.

"It's just that I've met someone else." He was wearing jean cutoff shorts and one of his testicles peeked out from the inside of his leg. He looked down at the ground. I felt like I was choking.

"Who is it? Is it someone from our class?" I kept staring at his ball.

It turned out the someone else was Nadine Horvath.

"But why her? What's so special about her?" Nadine Horvath was a nothing of a girl, a wispy, whiny drip with a bad perm.

"She needs me," he said, staring down at the scorched, brown grass.

Whatever the hell that meant it was a lie and I didn't believe him. I needed him so much more and he knew it. At that moment I hated him so much that I imagined tearing off his testicle and throwing it into the street, where maybe it would be run over by a big Chevy station wagon. I knew the real reason he was dumping me. He just didn't have the guts to tell me that he couldn't take the heat with my mother. If he really loved me, he would save me and take me away from everything, but he didn't really love me. My eyes stung with tears and the park smelled like baking dog shit.

I ran to my car and drove away without looking back at the boy who had just stomped on my heart. I screamed and sobbed, gripping the steering wheel. People stared at me through their car windows. I must have looked like a horror movie with the sound turned off.

At graduation, after the diplomas were handed out, my class sang the Beatles song "In My Life." I'm sure that to the faculty or other students it seemed an appropriate choice of a song for a group of people whose lives were about to change forever, and who had happy times to look back on, but to me, it sounded like a dirge.

Mother, decked out in one of her Chanel suits, took my picture in my white cap and gown beside Robbie in the pretty, tree-lined courtyard in front of the school, where the Beaver graduations always took place.

"Wendy, why don't you go ask Dylan to come over and I'll take a picture of you two on your big day."

Mother gestured to where he was standing with his family a few yards away. Conveniently for her, she had no recollection of her past bad behavior. That tape had been erased by white wine.

"Oh, Mother, please, I can't." I shot a pained look at Robbie, who pursed her lips but said nothing.

"Don't be ridiculous, he's standing right there." Mother pointed at him again. I glanced over and saw Nadine Horvath bounding up to him, looking like a frizzy-haired poodle.

"Please, don't point at him, and can you lower your voice?" I whispered, looking down at the ground at her feet.

"Why not? And who is that?" She sniffed in Nadine's direction.

"I'll tell you in the car, Mother."

Robbie and I started herding her toward the parking lot.

"What awful hair she has."

I looked over my shoulder at Dylan and wished he would turn to look at me, to make everything that was now so wrong right again. But he didn't. I turned away and we walked to the car.

"I'll drive," I said.

Once we were a safe distance away, I told Mother that Dylan had broken up with me and that he was dating the poodle girl now.

As she listened to me, her eyes became slits, and she lit up a cigarette. "I don't want you to worry about it." Her voice was low and conspiratorial, as if she were a criminal mastermind planning an assassination. "When we get home, I'll make some calls."

"Calls?" Calls from Mother had caused all this. "What are you going to do?"

"First, I'll make sure he's fired from his summer busboy job."

I eyed Robbie in the rearview mirror. She smirked and looked out the window, as if to say, *What did you expect?*

"Then I'll call your stepfather, who is still a very important man. I'm sure when he hears this, he'll be on the first plane to Boston with a baseball bat."

This was supposed to make me feel better. It was Mother's way of dealing with failed relationships—get revenge and screw the guy before he knew what had hit him.

"Please don't, Mother," I said.

But it was too late. Mother took my breakup personally. It was her story now—and she did not appreciate being dumped. Mother believed herself to be irresistible to all men—no matter their age. If they didn't make a pass or pay proper attention, they either had to be gay or mentally deficient. So if any man had the audacity to break up with her first, he would not be allowed to simply walk away. Not until he paid for it.

All I could hope was that Mother's white-wine IV would continue to drip, erase her memory of Dylan altogether, and spare me yet another humiliation.

chapter twelve

CANDYLAND

My summer job was hostessing at an upscale Chinese restaurant near my house called Joyce Chen. It was beautiful
inside, all gleaming wood and huge, ivory-carved drag-
ons in glass cases. I had no paid job experience, but the
guy who hired me was my age and had been doing work-
study at Joyce Chen all year to learn the business. Douglas
Kinoshita was a Japanese-American kid and wore his
black, straight hair long past his shoulders. He had one of
those fuzzy mustaches boys get before they start shaving.
Douglas always wore khakis and Top-Siders with an un-
tucked white or pink button-down shirt. He was barrel-
chested and densely built. He had recently gotten a hernia
from pushing off a refrigerator that had fallen on him.

The restaurant was a crazy place but not in a bad way.
All the waiters were Chinese men, and none of them could
say *Wendy*, so I was rechristened *Candy*. I thought this was

hilarious. It sounded like a stripper's name to me. The waiters all had other jobs, sometimes two, so they would take No-Doz or Dexatrim diet pills to make them speedy enough to work long days. As a result, they were all wound pretty tightly.

My first week at Joyce Chen, I was working a lunch shift when I saw one of the waiters, a man named Po, run through the front door spouting expletives.

"Lousy son of a bitch! I'll kill you, I swear!"

"Bad customer!" I heard another waiter announce as he motioned for all the servers on the floor to follow him out to the parking lot. Instantly, a brigade of manic Chinese men in dark blue jackets and name tags started scrambling, charging through the door like Keystone Kops. I followed to see what all the ruckus was about.

Outside, I watched Po hurl some change on the ground at the feet of the offending patron, who, I gathered from the way everyone was acting, had left an insufficient tip.

"You take this, Mr. Asshole! You need it more than me!"

The bad tipper blanched and started fumbling for his car keys, trying to open the door. Po lunged in the man's direction, throwing a punch at him. Po missed and his fist crunched into the man's car. Po screamed in pain.

"My family will starve because of you!" shouted Po, as the other waiters grabbed his flailing arms and started dragging him away. The terrified man took a few bills out of his wallet and threw them on the ground before jumping into his car and screeching away. One of the waiters fell back and picked up the money. I held the door open as they herded back into the restaurant.

"Thank you, Candy." They nodded as they filed past me. Then they started mumbling in Chinese. That summer, this parking-lot rumble happened weekly.

I enjoyed the camaraderie of the restaurant: we all ate together before work, and everyone laughed and joked with each other. It kind of reminded me of the theater, where you form a family of sorts away from home. Since I was headed to BU's school of liberal arts in the fall, I had pretty much given up on the idea of being an actress, but the restaurant provided that familiar feeling for me, which made me enjoy being there. And I had a role to play, of sorts, in Candy. Douglas had given me a box of cheongsam dresses that he'd found at the restaurant's warehouse, abandoned by a woman who had returned to China twenty years earlier. They fit me perfectly and were exquisitely beautiful, in vibrantly jewel-colored silks, and embroidered with flowers and birds. My favorite one was emerald green, with white lotus blossoms. Holding my menus at the hostess station, in my exotic garb, I imagined myself an Irish Anna May Wong, arranging the seating chart to my satisfaction. Besides the local Boston cognoscenti, there were politicians, Harvard professors, famous authors, and anchormen, who all followed me as I sashayed into the dining room, leading them to their tables. I greeted Peter Falk, seating him at the best table, and was sent in to help an inebriated Ginger Rogers in the ladies' restroom.

A few weeks after I started working there, Douglas sidled up to me, broadly grinning.

"What?" I said.

"Someone has a crush on you."

"You're kidding. Who?"

"A cook in the kitchen. He's been admiring you from afar." I was not allowed to go down into the kitchen. I had heard all sorts of wild rumors about illegal workers in the kitchen being kept in indentured servitude and forced to work for Joyce to win their freedom. I imagined a smoky room filled with sweaty men chained to stoves, stirring huge woks.

"What's his name?"

"Chang."

The only Chang I knew was the Siamese twin, Eng's brother.

"Actually, he's gotten a look at you and he's prepared to offer you five thousand dollars to marry him." Douglas chuckled; he seemed to be relishing his role as go-between.

"Five thousand dollars? But he doesn't even know me!"

"It's for a green card, silly. If he marries you, he can stay in this country legally."

"Oh." I actually considered this for a moment. I could marry Chang, get the money, and disappear. No one would have to know my name had once been Candy Chang. It almost sounded like a plan. "Can I meet him?"

"Sure. Come with me." Douglas took me through a series of dimly lit hallways that led to a black metal staircase. We then descended into what looked to me like the furnace room of the *Titanic*. Through thick steam I could see men in motion: cleavers chopping, knives slicing, woks banging on the tops of enormous ranges. We walked in between two rows of flaming burners. Douglas pointed to a skinny old man with no teeth.

"Chang, meet Candy. Candy, Chang."

"Hello," I croaked, coughing at the smoke enveloping us. Chang gave me a gummy smile.

Douglas then informed me that I would have to live with my new husband for a year to ensure his green-card status. Chang nodded and leered at me, perhaps envisioning our wedding night. He clearly saw himself as a catch and thought that I was getting the better end of the deal. I politely declined my first offer of marriage and my big chance to be Candy Chang.

"You're a riot," I said to Douglas as we walked back upstairs to the main floor.

"I thought you'd enjoy that." He grinned at me.

Douglas knew something was going on at my home when I showed up on his doorstep that summer at 2:00 a.m. with cuts all over my arms from trying to break into my house through a basement window. Mother had locked me out, but I had needed clean clothes for work and didn't want her to know how late I'd come home. They were superficial cuts. I stood in the kitchen while Douglas's mom put the small-size Band-Aids all over the insides of my arms and said nothing.

He may have suspected a few weeks earlier that all was not well with me when we had gone to see the Woody Allen movie *Interiors* and I had laughed my butt off through the whole thing. The scene where the mother, who is an insane perfectionist, duct-taped herself into her bedroom to gas herself was a hoot. I was still laughing when the lights came up at the end, after the mother succeeds in drowning herself in the ocean and her daughters all stare out the window at a tree. It cracked me up. People stared at us as we left the theater.

Douglas looked at me and said, "Are you hungry after all that laughing?" I was, so we drove down to Chinatown for wonton soup and spareribs.

While I counted down the days I had remaining at home, the conflict between my mother and my sister escalated into violence of such sensational proportions that it began to resemble a bad-girl prison movie. Mother was cast as the sadistic screw who was trying to crush the spirit of the wildcat juvie runaway—my sister.

The tension had started to snowball after Mother discovered my sister coming home at three in the morning. I was an expert at sneaking in, turning the headlights off before I pulled into the driveway, and knowing which steps on the staircase squeaked, but Robbie was less interested in covering her tracks, and it was her bad fortune to get caught.

"Where the hell have you been?!" Mother fumed, flicking on the lights in the foyer, my sister's keys still stuck in the door. I came to the top of the stairs to witness the scene.

"At a party, Mother, if you must know," Robbie replied somewhat archly.

"Do you know what time it is?" Mother shouted.

"What does it matter? You're usually passed out, anyway."

Mother slapped Robbie across the face, and my sister, without hesitating, slapped her right back.

Mother backed away, leaning against the wall for support while my sister walked by her and climbed the stairs.

From that moment on, it was war. Now they openly hated each other's guts and the gloves were off. Ever since our car ride back from the train station after my League audition, I had given up on trying to reach Mother. I just wanted to bide my time and stay below the radar until I could make my getaway. Robbie became determined to put a mirror up to Mother's face and show her all the ugliness inside her.

"You're a pathetic, sick-in-the-head drunk. All you do is drive people away with your toxic personality," Robin would coolly state.

This direct approach of my sister's pushed Mother's buttons big-time. Whereas I felt like I needed some directions and a map to try to understand Mother because she was like an alien from outer space, Robbie just told her to fuck off, that she hated her, and, worst of all, that she was insane. Then it was time for them to go a couple of rounds. I tried to intervene, but stopped after I got a bloody nose during one of their scuffles. A week after that, Robin pushed

Mother down the front stairs, just like in Mother's Kansas City bedtime story. Luckily or unluckily, it didn't succeed in killing her.

One day after working a lunch shift at the restaurant, I came home and heard a lot of thumping upstairs. My sister was supposed to be at her summer job at a nearby nursing home, where she was giving sponge baths to old people and emptying bedpans. Mother was taking a break from her summer job, writing her life story.

"Hello?" As I started up the stairs, I heard a crash. I rushed to Robbie's room and found my sister and my mother rolling around on the rug.

"You bitch!" my sister screamed. "I fucking hate you!"

Robbie's room was trashed. Clothing was strewn all over and a broken lamp was on the floor. A trickle of blood was coming from my sister's nose. They separated and scrambled to their feet to gear up for the next round, circling each other like wrestlers in the ring.

"I despise you, you little wretch!" Mother snarled back.

"Oh, yeah? Well, I wish you would just *die!*"

At this, Mother emitted a gurgling sound of rage and lunged at my sister. I watched them kicking and punching each other. *Maybe this is it,* I thought. *Maybe this will be the day they kill each other.* I waded into the fray, trying to pull Robbie away, and immediately caught a flying elbow in the eye. Mother's face was red and sweaty from trying to strangle her own daughter. My sister murderously bellowed and banged Mother's head against the floor. I ran to the window and, throwing it wide open, started to yell for help to anyone who might hear me.

"Help! Please, someone, help!" Right across the driveway I could see into the bedroom of our neighbor, a boy named Skip. Since our houses were so close together, I was sure he could hear everything that went on at our house above a certain decibel level, just like I could hear his Steely Dan records when he played them really loudly. Skip went to the local public high school and worked at a gas station. For both of these reasons, Mother disapproved of him. He spent a lot of time looking at Robbie from his window across the driveway, and I was pretty sure he had a crush on her. I screamed again, and Skip's head popped up into the window.

"Hey, what's up?" He was dressed in his gas station uniform and I think he'd been trying to take a nap. The name tag on his shirt said STEVE.

"They're fighting! I don't know what to do!"

"I'll be right there." And he was off.

I ran to the front door to meet him, and he followed me back upstairs, where they were still going at it big-house style. Skip said my sister's name, but she didn't hear him. Skip, who was bigger and no doubt stronger than my sister and my mother put together, spread his arms wide and grabbed Robbie around the waist, lifting her up in the air. She flailed her legs at Mother.

"Tell that crazy cow to leave me alone!" Robin yelled.

"You're coming with me right now." Skip turned, holding my sister in his arms, and charged from the room. I heard the front door slam a few moments later. Mother slowly stood up and smoothed her hair. She seemed unsure of what had just occurred. She had a scratch on her face.

"Well," said Mother, weaving her way back to her bedroom, "that boy and your sister deserve each other." Then she added haughtily, "He's just white trash."

I went next door to check on Robin. Skip's mom was never home because she had to work, and Skip didn't seem to have a dad. He let me in and led me into the living room. The walls were painted a dusky blue color, and the furniture was drab and colorless, giving the whole place a lifeless waiting-room feel. Robin was sitting in an armchair with a can of Fresca in her shaking hand. She was smoking one of Skip's Marlboro Reds. She flicked the ashes onto her jean leg and rubbed them in with her palm, then looked up at me.

"Are you okay?" I asked. I wanted to grab her and shake her and ask why she couldn't just keep her head down the way I did until she could make her escape.

"Yeah." She looked so small and alone sitting in that chair, like the little bird torn from the fence on her favorite music box.

I felt helpless to protect her now. What kind of a sister was I if I couldn't even keep her safe?

That weekend, Skip, our hero, invited us to a party. I think he was hoping Robbie might take notice of him after he'd rescued her. The party was all Belmont High kids, so we didn't really know anyone there. A friend of Skip's named Andrew was throwing the party because his parents were in the Bahamas. The house was pretty dark when we got there and packed with people. Cheap Trick blasted from the stereo speakers:

"Surrender, surrender, but don't give yourself away."

Robbie grabbed my hand and made a beeline for the kitchen. She opened the fridge and expertly grabbed two Rolling Rocks with one hand. She opened them and handed one to me. A guy asked her to dance and she said yes and disappeared into the dark with him. I took a sip of my beer and started to feel nervous because I was alone and surrounded by strangers. I looked around for Skip. The music was so loud I couldn't hear what anyone was saying. I drank more beer, which I didn't really like, but it gave me something to do while I stood there feeling as if people were staring at me.

Then, across the room, I saw Jack. Jack was a friend of Skip's I had met once before when Robbie and I bumped into them both at the record store in Belmont. He was cute, tall and blond with a thin face that made him look a little like Tom Petty. Jack used to go to the high school, but something had happened and his parents had sent him away to boarding school. Whatever had happened must have been bad, because it was Jesuit boarding school. I decided I wanted to find out. I took a big gulp of Rolling Rock and, so emboldened, walked over to him.

"Hi!" I shouted over the music. "I'm Wendy!"

He nodded and smiled at me. He had an easy smile, as

if he had it all figured out, but not in an arrogant way. He seemed older, even though I knew he was a year younger than me. He didn't say anything, so I took a sexy slug of my beer. It tasted like a swamp. He leaned over to talk into my ear. He smelled like soap and was wearing a flannel shirt that looked so soft I wanted to touch it. Around his throat was a puka-bead necklace.

"You want to go for a walk?" His lips brushed against my ear.

I nodded yes. I would have gone anywhere with him. The beer was bubbling through my head, making my temples throb. Jack took my hand and we started to move through the crush of people in the living room. I saw Robbie in the corner still dancing with the guy. Skip was slumped on a sofa watching them with a beer in his hand. Jack and I walked out the back sliding glass doors into the yard. He was still holding my hand as he led me down a slope to the bottom of the garden. We turned and looked back up at the house, which was dark against a night of stars. Jack put his hand under my hair; his fingers gently rubbed the nape of my neck. He drew me to him and kissed me. His breath smelled like cigarettes and beer but I didn't care, I liked it. When Jack kissed me, I suddenly wanted him to touch me everywhere at once and never stop. He pulled me down onto the grass next to him and whispered in my ear, and again I felt his lips there.

"Do you want me to show you something?"

Yes, I thought, *yes, please.* "What?"

"Lie down." He looked down at my jeans and undid

them. Then he pulled my jeans and my underwear down. The blood was pounding in my ears and I felt tingly all over, as if fingertips were softly drumming my face. I looked up into the sky. Then he put his mouth on me between my legs and it felt wet and warm. I looked at the stars, then down at the top of his head. I wondered how long it would last— the heat and the heaviness of his body on top of me, pressing me against the ground. He was like a mountain on me, and the stars rushed into my head. I thought about when I flew in my dreams, that moment when my feet would lift off the ground and I would soar above the trees and look down at the tiny town below. I was flying with nothing but air around me.

"Oh my God."

He stopped, looked at me, and smiled. I caught my breath.

"We should go back," he said, offering me a hand up.

"Why did you do that?"

"I don't know." He pushed my hair back behind my ear and looked me in the eye. "You just looked so fucking sad."

He took my hand as we walked back into the house, like he was with me, as if I were his girlfriend—which, judging from what had just happened, I hoped I was. People were looking at us. Jack and I moved into the swaying crowd of kids, who were slow-dancing on the rug, now littered with potato chips and beer cans. We held each other and moved back and forth to the music. I buried my face in his shirt and inhaled. He smelled like fresh air.

The rest of that summer, I went to work at the restaurant during the day, then I'd go out with Jack at night. Sometimes he would pick me up from work in his white VW Beetle. We didn't really go anywhere; we would just drive around Belmont. It seemed exotic to me that Jack had lived in Belmont his entire life, since I hadn't grown up anywhere. He knew all the best places to go. Sometimes we'd climb the fence around the local swimming pool, strip off our clothes, and float on our backs in the water, looking up at the night sky.

Another place he liked to take me was off a little dirt road at the top of a hill where you could see the whole city of Boston. It was a kind of secret place that he said not many people knew about. He used to come here with his friends from school, get high, and just look at the lights. Sometimes we would park there, sit on the hood of the car, drink beers, and talk. I made him laugh with stories about the restaurant and my alter ego, Candy. He told me about growing up in Belmont, and his school in New Hampshire, which he liked.

"So why did your parents send you to boarding school?"

He handed me a beer and I took a sip. I found I had acquired a taste for it since making Jack's acquaintance.

"You know, I started hanging out with all these stoner kids and my grades went into the crapper. My mom and dad got really upset with me. They were worried, and I was just fucking up." He looked out over the city and drank his beer.

"So then what happened?"

"They basically pulled me out in the middle of the year and sent me to Proctor. I actually really like it."

"What's Catholic school like?"

"Catholic school? Jesus, who told you that?" He laughed and snorted some beer out of his nose, which he wiped on his sleeve. "It's not Catholic. I do have a teacher who is a Jesuit priest, and he's a very cool guy. We talk a lot." He told me he was thinking about becoming a priest. I thought that was sexy.

Then I explained to him that I could never, ever, have him over to my house, because my mother was certifiably insane, and that anyone who got close to me would get dragged into the shit show that defined my home life. Robbie and I had recently found Mother passed out on the kitchen floor with a huge bump on her forehead. By the time the ambulance arrived, she had come to. She won over the paramedics, who were too taken by her to notice that she was in her stained nightdress and reeked of Mondavi. They bandaged her head and she bobbed around looking like a wizened Sabu.

"Well, in that case I don't want to meet her. She doesn't sound anything like you." He reached over and pulled me next to him, hugging me close. We looked at the lights.

"So you'll have to be my secret love." I smiled into his eyes.

"Fine with me."

Our dates ended with my going back to his house, where we did it on a double bed in his basement while his parents and kid sister slept upstairs. When I sneaked back into my house, I could usually count on Mother's being fairly sedated, and a fan in the window covered up any noise I might make on the stairs.

One night, Jack drove me home at five in the morning. I kissed him good-bye and tiptoed up the driveway to the back stairs. I came around the corner of the house and was horrified to see Mother sitting on the back stairs in her nightgown, smoking a cigarette.

She stared at me disdainfully. "You know, Wendy, you can't fool me."

I didn't know what to say, so I kept quiet.

"I have an eye in the back of my head. I can always see you, wherever you are." She stood up, tossing her cigarette butt into the trees. "I am all-knowing and all-seeing." She regarded me with an air of superiority and, turning, walked up the steps and back into the house.

Even though I was eighteen, and technically a grown-up, Mother could still fill me with her own particular brand of fear. While her drunken tirades and throwing of furniture were intimidating and scary, it was her cryptic spookiness and talent for surprise that allowed her to retain a power over me.

As we neared the end of the summer, I started to feel a building excitement over my looming departure for school, and supreme guilt over leaving my sister behind. A part of me felt enormous relief, knowing that my escape was imminent, but I was deeply concerned about leaving Robbie with our mother the shrike. My sister had a gift for getting under Mother's skin, putting out the fire with gasoline.

"I mean, what are you supposed to do?" Robin snorted. "Stay home and babysit me?" We were in her room and she was painting her fingernails fire-engine red. I just bit mine while we talked.

"I'm just worried, that's all."

"Well, don't be. I can take care of myself." I knew she was tougher, and braver than me certainly. She fanned her fingers in the air to dry her polish.

"Promise me you'll call if the shit hits the fan."

"Okay . . . . Gee, I wonder when that will be?" She looked at her watch theatrically, then laughed.

"No, really, be serious."

"Lighten up! You should be happy you're being set free from this nuthouse." She smiled and I felt a hair better.

A few days before my departure, Mother started negotiating with me. She tried to bribe me with the promise of a new car if I agreed to live at home. I didn't need a car at BU, and where she thought the money for a new car would come from, I had no idea. So I held firm in my resolve to live on campus. If across town was as far as I could get, then so be it.

"Don't forget, Wendy, who's paying for you to go to college."

"Yes, Mother."

Although Mother behaved as if she were picking up the tab for my college education, she was not footing the bill.

The small trust fund my grandfather had left my sister and me to pay for college was still intact. Mother had been able to divert some of the interest for her own use, but the bulk of it remained at the bank in Kansas City. I didn't care about the money except the part that allowed me to finally leave home. After I escaped her clutches, she could have the rest. It was a small price to pay.

I went over to Jack's house to say good-bye. He was leaving the next day to go back to boarding school for his senior year. His mom let me in and told me he was up in his room packing his trunk.

"I'll miss you," I said as I watched him fold his clothes and ball up his socks.

"No, you won't." He shot me a killer smile. "You'll be too busy."

It was true that I would miss him, but I was also excited about going to college, where I thought my life would finally begin and become exciting in ways not related to suicide notes and speeding cars.

"We'll be really far apart from each other, so I don't want you to feel bad if you meet somebody else," he said.

I wanted him to be upset that we weren't going to see each other for a while. But he was being so goddamn grown-up about it.

"I won't. Meet someone else, I mean."

"You're going to meet a lot of people. It's a big school."

"You're not a priest yet, okay? So stop trying to get rid of me."

I walked over to him and he put his arms around me. He still smelled like soap and trees, I thought, as we kissed. We promised to see each other at the Thanksgiving break. He gave me the number of the hall phone outside his dorm room.

"Good-bye, Candy," he said.

chapter thirteen

BURNING DOWN THE HOUSE

The day I left for BU happened to coincide with Mother's fortieth birthday. On top of that, Pop, finished with Mother's hysterical phone calls and pleas for cash, finally severed all ties with her by canceling the life insurance policy of which he had made her the beneficiary. It all hit her like a falling piano: she was middle-aged, friendless, manless, broke, and her eldest was leaving the nest. She was stunned into a catatonic silence. Robbie sat in the backseat, smiling and looking out the window as if she were sightseeing in some beautiful tropical paradise.

When Mother dropped me off outside my dorm, she stayed behind the wheel, frozen like a corpse with a lit cigarette. Robbie helped me unload my stuff onto the pavement. I embraced my sister and strongly resisted the desire to dance a jig right there on the sidewalk.

"Good-bye, Mother!" I bent down and smiled at her through the window. She didn't look at me as the car slowly pulled away from the curb. Robbie sat in the front, doing a Queen Elizabeth wave at me as the car crawled down the street at a hearselike pace.

Surrounded by tearful parents hugging their children beside laundry baskets filled with alarm clocks and lamps and footballs, I watched the car disappear around the corner—and I started to laugh. The kind of giddy laugh that you hear in casinos after a win. Or in my case, in a dark theater watching a Woody Allen movie. I was free.

My housing at BU was in a brownstone on a quiet narrow street behind Commonwealth Avenue named Buswell Street. My roommate, Julie, was from Chicago and was studying painting at the school for the arts. She was a very sweet, sunny, uncomplicated girl with adoring, supportive parents, who also happened to be enormously wealthy. So she was basically the polar opposite of me.

As the anti-me, Julie would spring from bed in the morning, happy to be alive, drink a cup of herbal tea, and dash off to class. While Julie's goal of being a painter was in front of her, mine—escaping my mother—was behind me. I slept until noon, made myself an instant coffee, then strolled to one of the English or theater classes I'd signed up for from the catalog with barely a glance. Finally sprung from the confines of the Snake Pit, I let my newfound freedom go to my head. Like Auntie Mame said in the movie, "Life is a banquet and most poor suckers are starving to death." I was famished, and now I was making up for lost time.

I ate at the vegetarian dining hall, not for the food but for the company. Everyone there was cool and doing something interesting. Greg and Craig were in the acting program, Alice was studying the violin, and Hugh wanted to be a writer. I wanted to be more like them, more of a bohemian. I permed my long blond hair into a mass of kinky curls like Alice, who looked like Stevie Nicks. Alice ran around in an old tuxedo jacket, so I started shopping in thrift stores for secondhand stuff. I wore anything that would make me look like one of my fellow gypsies—dangly seashell earrings, a ratty cardigan, harem pants, tie-dyed scarves, preferably with holes in them. I started smoking those stinky clove cigarettes, Djarums. Weekends we would all gather at Craig and Greg's (they had the biggest place) and listen to jazz and dance and play the bongos. Saturday nights we'd get dressed up and go to the midnight *Rocky Horror Picture Show* at the Harvard Square Theatre. I felt free and the happiest I'd been since London.

Barely two weeks into my own personal *La Dolce Vita*, I awoke in the middle of the night to knocking on my door and my sister's distraught voice coming from the hallway.

"Wendy, open up. Please." Her voice was shaking.

"What is it? What's going on?" I let her in, trying to whisper to keep from waking my roommate. Robin's face was shiny with tears.

"She tried to set fire to my room." Robin cleared her throat, something she always did when she was upset and trying not to lose it.

"Jesus."

"She was drunk and she grabbed this shirt off the floor and lit it on fire with a Bic lighter."

"Are you hurt?" By this time, Julie had got out of bed and was standing next to mine. She turned on the little lamp on my bedside table.

"She tried to throw the shirt at me, but it landed on top of my stereo and it started to smoke and melt. I grabbed it and ran to the bathroom and threw it in the toilet but the curtains caught on fire."

"What's going on?" Julie asked. I gave her the lowdown. "Wow. So she's really nuts."

I nodded. Together we made a bed on the floor for Robin with extra blankets and pillows.

"Have you ever tried just talking to her?" Julie asked.

I was always asked this question by people who meant well but had no idea what it was like dealing with the highly irrational. They wondered why I couldn't just bring all this to a halt with a few well-chosen words. I wanted to explain that I was a teenager, not Carl Jung or a lion tamer. You couldn't just read I'm OK, You're OK and grasp this situation. I couldn't heal my mother's wounded Inner Child, no matter how many pop-psychology books I read. The world Robbie and I lived in was like a parallel universe, and unless you'd been there, you couldn't possibly fathom it. Even then, Mother's ability to turn off the crazy and pour on the charm left people, like the para-medics, unaware of what was really going on.

I smiled at Julie and assured her that it didn't work

that way. Robbie and I were alone inside our world of understanding. I suppose in a way my childhood practice of shielding my sister from the truth, and later keeping it from the world, derived from Mother's example. But at least I was trying to use it for good. I looked down to see my sister already asleep with the covers pulled over her head.

The next day, I called Dr. Keylor. I hadn't seen her since graduating from high school, but I was still paying off my bill. I told her what had happened. Dr. Keylor spoke in an unruffled tone, but I could hear the concern in her voice. I held the telephone in between me and Robbie so she could hear.

"If you believe that your mother is a danger to others or to herself, I think you should seriously consider having her committed."

"You mean like a hospital?" I imagined Mother wrapped in a straitjacket, spouting expletives as she was stuffed into an ambulance, while the neighbors stood around watching. Like her own mother being taken away on a stretcher but without the reassuring terminal diagnosis.

"Yes, where she might be able to get some help. Talk it over with your sister. I can help you take the necessary steps."

I thanked Dr. Keylor and hung up the phone.

"Well, she is dangerous," Robin said, "but putting her in some place?" Robin ran her index finger across her throat. Committing her seemed even more scary because of what she would do to us when she got out. She'd hunt us down and kill us like some deranged convict, escaped to wreak vengeance on her accusers. We'd have to go into Witness Protection.

I wondered what else I could do—who else could I call?

I walked to Commonwealth Avenue and called my step-father collect from a pay phone. Pop had always rescued us before—from bad hotels, bankruptcy, insanity. But this time he told me he couldn't do it. Things had deteriorated so much with Mother that he might have to change his phone number. She'd even called his other ex-wives. He no longer had any control over her.

It wasn't the answer I'd wanted, but after everything I'd seen, I understood. I thanked him anyway and asked him why he'd stuck around for so long, paying our private-school tuitions, fees for summer camp in Switzerland, and class trips to Africa.

"Dearie," he said, "it is probably the nicest thing I've ever done."

My sister started camping out at friends' houses, with me in the small room I shared with Julie, or with anyone we could find who had room for her for a few days. For a month, she lived in my friend Alison Martin's large walk-in closet in her Boston College dorm room. Robin would go back home when things had blown over.

Some days it felt like I hadn't really escaped at all. I could still feel my mother's tentacles reaching through the phone line, trying to drag me back into the darkness. My phone would ring and ring and I didn't always pick it up. Sometimes I'd pick up the receiver on the twenty-fifth ring and drop it back into the cradle. Then, other days I was almost happy: I was getting by in my classes, and I wasn't living at home. Robbie came and went when she needed to, and Douglas would drop by some nights and take me to our favorite place in Chinatown, King Fung, for wonton soup.

We drove down to Chinatown in the big white van he drove for the restaurant, which smelled of fish. We ate wonton soup in silence. I'd had an easy familiarity with Douglas from the first time we'd met. It was like discovering a brother I didn't know I had. We both had fathers who had disappeared: mine into another family somewhere in the Midwest, and his into the arms of a mistress in Japan. I felt that he would have done anything for me. We didn't need to talk about it. It was just there on the table like the soy sauce.

One day, close to Thanksgiving break, I was studying for a history test when the phone rang and rang for what seemed like ten minutes.

Exasperated, I picked it up. "Hello, Mother." I didn't see any point in pretending I didn't know who it was.

"I simply cannot control your sister. She's run off again and I'm thinking of calling the police." At least she sounded sober.

"Please don't do that, Mother. I'm sure I can find her. And would you mind not calling me quite so much?"

"Excuse me?" She assumed her imperious tone. I had said the wrong thing.

"It's just that it makes it hard to concentrate on my schoolwork."

Silence. Shit. I knew I had blown it, so I just waited for the recoil.

"Oh. I see. Your life is so much more important than mine. You're busy and I'm bothering you."

"I don't mean that."

"You know something, Wendy? If you think that what I'm doing is easy—raising your impossible sister—then you can just stay at college for all I care."

I listened to her smoke for a while.

"I only meant that—"

"Don't bother coming home for Thanksgiving." She hung up on me.

It had been a year since our Thanksgiving trip to the emergency room, so Robbie and I were relieved to get a break from the funny farm. She headed for her friend Beth's house for a safe and incident-free holiday, and I went to Jack's house in Belmont. I had only had time to call him once since I had started college, and he had written to me a few times. He had explained the whole thing to his parents, who were nice and incredibly normal. Compared to my house, I felt as if I were celebrating Thanksgiving on Planet Corny, but I loved every second of it. Jack's family and their friends chatted and drank eggnog. The men wore jackets with tartan ties, the women dressed in kilts and Fair Isle sweaters, and the little girls wore party dresses. Jack gave a spontaneous prayer of thanks before the feast. I looked at him in his blazer and tie in the candlelight talking about love, and I thought, *Maybe he will be a priest. A very cute priest.*

After dinner, Jack and I stayed up late, listening to Genesis records in the living room. Then he said good night to me in a loud voice. I went downstairs and he went to his room. Then he snuck down later and met me on the bed in the basement.

I helped him pack up his trunk before he went back to school. I had a feeling of finality this time, watching him get ready to go. I cared about him, but we were so far apart. I felt I couldn't burden him with my ongoing family wars and that it wasn't fair for me to depend on him, that somehow he was no longer mine. We spoke on the phone a few times after that, but it felt strained and disconnected somehow. We broke up before Christmas. I sensed that he might have met someone else, but if he did, he never told me. I was sad but not brokenhearted as I had been the last time. It seemed possible to love someone and be loved without catastrophe and pain occurring—this realization gave me hope.

Back at the Snake Pit, the pattern became this: My sister started running away so often that, before she could, Mother would throw her out of the house. When she left, Mother would call the police and tell them Robin had run away and stolen the Subaru. The police made it clear they had better things to do than flag down my sister on Belmont High Street and bring her home. It looked as if without me as a buffer or a distraction, it became impossible for my mother to leave my sister alone—like a little kid with a scab she can't stop picking at. For Robbie, the only choices were fight or flight, and neither was a good one.

I was home one weekend and noticed that my sister's bedroom door was covered with an Indian-print tablecloth. When I looked underneath, I saw that the whole center panel of the door was missing and there were gashes in the wood. I asked Robbie what had happened.

She had come home from school to find Mother in her room, going through her drawers.

"What are you doing?" my sister asked.

"Don't you keep a diary? I thought all teenage girls kept diaries." Mother kept rummaging.

"Why would I write my private thoughts down when you would just read them? I live with you. I don't need to write about it. And this is *my* room."

Mother strode out the door. My sister locked the door after her. Minutes later, a loud thwacking sounded on the other side of the door as Mother chopped it in with an ax.

"There are no locked doors in this house, young lady!" Mother boomed from the hall, while Robin screamed and covered her ears and wood chips flew all over.

"So I put the Indian print over it. I mean, I think it looks nice, you know?" Robin shrugged.

I looked around Robbie's room. The burn marks on the stereo, the scorch marks on the rug, the axed-in door, the little broken-music-box shelf. It was pathetic, and clearly time for me to assume my role as hostage negotiator and attempt to secure my sister's release. I started by finding the ax in the garage and hiding it behind some rhododendron bushes in the backyard.

Robbie had a friend from high school, a pale, sad-faced girl named Hope, who was estranged from her family and living in a big old house with some other castaway children. My sister wanted to join them, but without Mother's agreement it wouldn't be possible. My job was to convince my mother that my sister should move into this house for the last half of her senior year of high school. Otherwise, I pointed out, they would wind up killing each other and someone might end up in jail. Robin was seventeen, after all, and could definitely take care of herself. Mother said nothing and just gave me the hairy eyeball I had seen so many times before. I knew that the most important thing to Mother in this situation was her exoneration from any guilt or responsibility, followed closely by a large helping of groveling dished out by my sister. Robin was so desperate to go I thought she'd agree to any terms.

On her last day at home, we stood in the driveway to play out Robin's departure scene like actors in a movie, hoping the only take we had went well.

"Just remember, Robin, that you are not moving out. I am throwing you out because you are an out-of-control, disobedient child who has no appreciation for anything I've ever given you," Mother began.

I held my breath. Robin folded her arms across her chest. "Okay."

"You have proven yourself to be undeserving of my patience and my generosity."

And let's not forget awesome mothering skills, I thought as I watched the scene.

"Even if you asked me to stay, I would have to say no."

I glanced nervously over at Robbie. I could see her coming to a boil. I prayed she could keep it together.

"Well, I guess I can't ask then. I'll just take my things and go," she said.

"Aren't you even going to apologize to me for what you've done?"

I could tell Mother had a wicked hangover and her voice shook. This was the deal breaker; without an apology, everything would go nuclear. I chewed the inside of my lip, waiting.

Robin cleared her throat a few times, looking down at the gravel, then said, "Sorry."

And that was it. My sister would never again be under the same roof as my mother.

We loaded a suitcase and the few boxes Robin had been allowed to take into the Subaru, and we drove to her new home in Jamaica Plain. I thought it was a bit grim. The paint was peeling, the furniture tatty, and Robin's new roommate Hope seemed totally depressed about her life. But there was plenty of room and Robin was away from Mother. Safe. I kissed my sister good-bye and took the T back to school.

I finished out my year at college that May with no great distinction, though I had managed to get my grades up to B's and one C by the end of the year. My crowd at school was moving on. Craig and Greg were going to Juilliard. My roommate, Julie, was transferring to the School of Visual Arts in New York City. Lacking funds for a summer rental, I was going home and hoped Douglas would give me my old job back.

I saw my sister only periodically. We had always been so close, a team united against you-know-who, but all of a sudden our relationship became strained and distant. She acted as if I had abandoned her, and I felt that she had chosen her newfound friends over me. Her roommates seemed to be her new family, and the family didn't include me. When I went over to her place, I imagined that everyone was staring at me and that Robin had told them what a weasel I was. I felt guilty about all the time I had spent away. I hadn't been there to help her because I was too busy trying to live my own life. I was a selfish bitch just like Mother had been telling me all these years.

Maybe all this weirdness between us was what made me start sneaking Robin's stuff out of her room and taking it over to her new house. She had been allowed to take very little with her. So, a few weeks before her graduation from Beaver, I drove over one evening with a box of records and books and a shopping bag of her clothes. I knocked on the front door, and Robin's roommate Hope answered. Instead of inviting me in, she stood in the doorway. Her lank, mousy brown hair framed her long, thin face, which had no expression at all.

"Yes?" It seemed to me that she was pretending that she didn't know who I was. I shifted the box onto my other knee. The shopping bag was hanging on my arm. It was heavy but Hope didn't notice.

"Hi, it's me, Robin's sister? Is she here?"

"I'll go see."

Hope padded across the foyer and started up a rickety staircase, leaving the door open. I invited myself in, closing the front door with my foot and dropping the box onto a chair and the bag on the floor. Robin came down the stairs a minute later, dressed in a bathrobe, her face damp from the shower and her hair wrapped in a towel. She was followed by Hope, who then sat on the stairs watching us. My sister had a blank look similar to Hope's; I couldn't tell if she was glad to see me or sorry that I came. Robin looked up at Hope a few times, as if they were exchanging thoughts telepathically. This made me feel resentful and threatened.

"I snuck this stuff out. I don't think she'll notice."

We just stood there in the hallway, looking at one another. I shot Hope a dirty look. I pointed to the box on the chair and Robin crossed over to it, flipping through the records, and peered into the shopping bag.

"Thanks," Robin said with a shrug, like it was no big deal. This, along with the presence of Hope as a kind of chaperone or witness to the proceedings, pissed me off. I thought of how Mother had put all of Robbie's things in garbage bags and stripped the room. It already looked as if she had never been there. I was sticking my neck out and my sister couldn't care less.

"Well," I replied, trying to cover my feelings of anger and awkwardness, "I thought you might like to have them." *I'm trying to help you, stupid*, I wanted to say. She had been my closest friend, playmate, the person with whom I shared my secrets. We had been through the shit together. Now it was as if we were strangers. All our games, dreams, nicknames, shot to hell. I had thought taking her stuff to her would make her happy, but it just made me look like a kiss-ass.

Robin shoved her hands deep into her pockets. "You coming to the graduation?" I detected a faint smile.

"Sure. I'll be there."

"Okay. Dinner's ready so we have to go." Robin gestured to some other room in the house. I hadn't got past the hall-way. I said good-bye and left.

We. It was a different *we* now.

On the day of Robin's graduation from high school, I knocked politely on Mother's bedroom door to ask if she was coming. There was no answer. I took that as a no. About fifteen minutes later, dressed and running late, I was load-ing a few boxes of Robbie's stuff into the Subaru when sud-denly Mother appeared, dressed in her nightgown, dragging two of the big black garbage bags from Robin's room toward her car. She flung the car door open, stuffed the bags inside, and turned to face me. Her greasy hair hung around her face, which was distorted and exaggerated like a mask in a Japanese play.

"You're not going to that fucking ceremony for that little bitch!" she screamed.

I took a step back, but in seconds she was across the lawn, standing right in front of me. Before I knew what was happening, she snatched my car keys away and threw them into the bushes in front of the house. She leapt into her car and raced away, the bottom of the blue nightgown caught in the door and dragging in the street.

As her car disappeared, I began to panic. I hunted for the keys on my hands and knees, crawling under the bushes in my white dress. It took me about five minutes, but I found them. I ran to the Subaru and drove to school as fast as I could.

By the time I arrived, the ceremony was over. This seemed odd to me as it should have lasted at least an hour and would normally still have been going on. As I walked up the tree-lined, curved driveway in front of the main building where the ceremony was held, I noticed that people were staring at me in a queer way. Then I saw Mr. Valentine coming toward me with a stricken look on his face, like the mask of tragedy that quickly changed to comedy—an artificially cheerful smile. He took my arm and steered me toward the school auditorium, where the reception was being held.

"I want you to go and stand next to your sister right now and pretend that nothing is wrong," he said in a low voice.

I suddenly felt like I had swallowed an anvil and my ears

started to tingle. I turned to him, as I had many times before for direction: Where should I go? What should I feel? But this was real life and not the stage. I asked him what had happened, and he pulled me into a doorway and told me with a big smile on his face, so no one would suspect he was giving me bad news.

While I was crawling around in the dirt under the bushes looking for my keys, Mother (apparently having changed her mind about attending my sister's graduation) drove directly to the school. When she got to the gates, she honked her horn to announce her arrival, then drove her car up the driveway, past all the parents, faculty, and students sitting on folding chairs in the courtyard listening to the headmaster's speech, and stopped right in front of the dais. People looked at each other, confused by the sudden appearance of this petite woman in her car with a cigarette holder sticking out of her mouth. No one moved. The headmaster stopped speaking. Mother got out, yanked her muddy nightgown hem free of the door, and flicked her ash.

I could just imagine the ripple of shocked chatter from the audience observing the scene.

"Who on earth is that?" muttered Beatrice Kleppner, whose son Paul was graduating that day.

"I don't know, dear," said her husband, Daniel, "but she's in her nightdress."

Tippy Nauts, the school secretary, who had offered to man the phones that day, was watching all this in horror from the small window in her office. *Good Lord*, she realized,

*it's that awful Rea woman, the one who smokes in the audito-
rium.* Tippy quickly picked up the telephone and called the
Brookline police.

"Do you think she was invited?" hissed Erica Labalme
behind her program to her husband, Hector.

"Perhaps she's lost," Hector replied foggily.

With all eyes upon her, Mother proceeded to deposit
the garbage bags, filled with my sister's things, in front of
the podium. A sea of faces stared. It wasn't just your run-of-
the-mill "I'm going to rain on your parade" moment, it was a
huge "Fuck you, I am going to ruin your life" moment.

My mother probably saw it as her crowning achievement,
an Oscar-worthy humiliation of my sister. Unfortunately for
her, no one else did. When Mother attempted to get back in
her car, she was quickly subdued by a few of the more strap-
ping fathers present.

"Don't you dare touch me!" Mother had screamed as she
tried to twist herself free.

"Calm yourself, madam," Hector said, holding her, while
another man took away her cigarette holder before somebody got burned.

"Yeah, take it easy," the man said, crushing the cigarette
under his shoe. When the police arrived, she was arrested
and led away handcuffed, screaming in her nightgown.

"So go over there and act natural," Mr. V said.

Act natural, I thought blankly, and made my way as if

underwater to stand next to my sister in the auditorium. She was next to a table that had a plate of cookies on it, staring straight ahead. I stood next to her with an idiotic smile on my face and felt that an imaginary circle was around us that no one dared come into for fear of catching some disfiguring disease. Everyone seemed to be safely keeping their distance, except for Mr. V, who stood inside the circle nervously eating all the cookies off the plate.

I explained what had happened, Mother throwing the keys and my hunt for them. Robin listened to what I had to say and told me it wasn't my fault. I think she was in shock, retreating into some other place in her mind where none of this had occurred. I felt ashamed about not having been there to stop it. Later, Robbie went to her home and I went to mine.

The police brought Mother home that evening. When I confronted her, she just ranted about what the police had done to her.

"They humiliated me!"

"How could you do such a horrible thing?"

"And they hurt me. Look at my wrists. They handcuffed me!"

"Answer me. Why?" But she didn't have an answer. It was like trying to ask Godzilla why he destroyed Tokyo.

"And then they raped me!" She wept and climbed the stairs to her room.

Once again, she failed to see that what she had done had injured someone else—her own daughter—so deeply. She only saw the red marks on her own arms.

The next day, I drove her out to school so we could pick up her car. It was parked next to the tennis courts where the police had left it. We rode in silence.

In therapy, Dr. Keylor had encouraged me to try to see the good and the bad in my mother, her strengths and weaknesses. Her weakness seemed to be her diseased mind, but I had to say her strong suit was making herself the center of attention.

At the end of the summer, I drove Robin to the airport to put her on a plane to Missouri, where she would be attending Stephens College. I was happy that, after all this time, it was Robbie who truly ended up escaping. We were sisters, and that bond connected us, but she was the sister who had received the brunt of our shared circumstance. I had survivor's guilt about being passed over while Mother campaigned so virulently to extinguish my sister's spirit. Now, Robbie was finally free and going a thousand miles away. She deserved it.

I walked with her to the gate.

"I don't get it." She looked at me, shaking her head.

"What?"

"I don't understand why you stay. I mean, you know it's just going to be her same old shit over and over, right?"

"Yeah, I guess." I shrugged, not knowing what else to say. I hugged her and told her to write to me when she got there.

"You know what your problem is?" she said, turning back from the gangway. "You're too fucking *nice*."

chapter fourteen

AA AND BEYOND

Since the whole graduation travesty, I was sure that Mother was unable to care for herself, and I decided to live at home instead of moving back to the dorms for my sophomore year. I had convinced myself that Mother needed me. What I failed to understand is that people as delusional as Mother are far stronger than they appear and don't need any assistance. But I was a nineteen-year-old idiot who'd been playing the role of the enabling eldest daughter to Mother's Joan Crawford for so long, I didn't know any other way of life. I was thinking that I might have let Robin down, but I could still be there to fish Mother out of the Charles River or go pick her up at the police station if she was arrested again.

I told Mother that there was one condition: if I stayed, she would have to attend Alcoholics Anonymous meetings. I considered this a stroke of genius on my part. Using emotional blackmail, I almost felt like Mother's worthy adversary. *Touché! I can beat you at this game,* I thought. Instead of being outraged at this suggestion, Mother greeted it with a Zen-like calm.

"If that's what makes you happy, Wendy." She peered at me innocently over her fully loaded ashtray. I was wary of her quiet acceptance, but I'd take whatever I could get.

As an extra piece of life insurance, I invited my friend Amy from next door at Buswell Street to move into Robin's room. Amy was transferring out of BU to Emerson College and needed a place to stay until she found an apartment near campus. I thought Mother would like the extra money, and I also wanted the protection of having someone else around. I thought that with regular AA attendance and a lodger who had never seen her dark side, Mother might actually behave herself and would be less likely to wade into the deep end.

Amy, in addition to going to school, worked nights at a local radio station called WBCN, answering the request line. Amy had introduced me to the Boston music scene. At BU, she would sometimes stop by late at night and invite me to a show at hot clubs like the Rat or the Paradise. Amy got her name on a lot of guest lists, so I got to see Boston bands with names like Human Sexual Response, Mission of Burma, and La Peste. If there was a knock on my door after eleven at night, I knew it was Amy.

"Hey, I got my name at the door tonight at Bunratty's. Want to go?"

My roommate was the early-to-bed type, and I jumped

at the chance to get out of my tiny room and experience some nightlife.

Amy was unlike anyone else I had ever met or been friends with. She was a Jewish girl from Long Island with a wild mane of brown hair and a tattoo on her ass. She had a weakness for Rastafarians, drove a big brown Camaro, and smoked Parliaments. Amy was a club girl and a night owl, but kind of a loner like me.

She moved into Robin's room and I felt better just knowing someone else was there.

Mother's first AA meeting was at Belmont Hospital near our house. I decided to drive her to make sure she was going; after the rock-on-the-fender incident, I wasn't taking any chances. She sat in the car, expressionless like a smoking sphinx. We walked through the parking lot in silence and into a room painted the color of old people's teeth, with overhead fluorescent lighting. I walked her up to the front row of folding chairs where she could sit with all the other alcoholics, then took a seat in the very back of the room where I imagined the nondrunks sat. The first thing I noticed was that everyone was smoking. *Good, she'll fit right in,* I thought. Then a grizzled man in his seventies with a bumpy, red nose got up and introduced himself to the crowd.

"Hello, my name is Howard and I'm an alcoholic."

"Hello, Howard," everyone echoed back.

Howard had been a reporter at the *Boston Globe* for thirty years and had spent all his free time in the local bar, knocking back the Cutty Sarks while he waited for the big stories to break. He talked wistfully about the cops dragging the city for the Boston Strangler, the bank robberies and the fires he had covered, and I couldn't help thinking that he seemed to really miss drinking. In fact, my impression of all the people who spoke was that they were nostalgic about the good old days when they were living much more exciting lives, boozing it up. *Never mind,* I thought, *I got her here, so let's make the best of it.* The meeting ended with more smoking, and coffee was served in Styrofoam cups. Mother seemed to be enjoying herself, puffing up a storm cloud of cigarette smoke, and working a room of people who didn't know she had a police record.

I halfheartedly enrolled in some classes, which I halfheartedly attended. In my French Existentialist Cinema class, my teacher looked like Mr. Death. He always wore black, was thin with waxy white skin, and liked to rant with his arms raised over his head about how badly the French had behaved during World War II.

"Don't you see? They behaved like pigs! They worship people like Maurice Chevalier and Jerry Lewis! So utterly banal!"

I went to my Introduction to Creative Writing class, but only on the days that my work wasn't being read. It was easy to be invisible in this way. My other two classes were art history and a costume class in which I did the minimum of work, so I was barely passing them. Living in the house with Mother made me feel sad and tired, and a kind of heaviness soaked into my bones. I missed my sister, and walking past her old room reminded me of her absence and all the turmoil that had occurred there. Everything I normally did—walking up the stairs, putting the dishes away, hanging up my coat—seemed to take more energy than I possessed. Except for Amy, I had no friends at school and couldn't seem to make new ones. Sometimes, in the evenings at the dinner table, I felt like Mother's paid companion, a forlorn girl in a Victorian novel who has to sit with an old lady and keep her company.

At her next AA meeting, Mother was given a sponsor, a plain woman named Carol, who was supposed to check up on Mother, and whom she could call if she felt she was going to start drinking again. Carol had been a librarian until excessive drinking had caused her to be fired from her job. Carol dutifully phoned my mother every evening and they had a nice chat.

About two weeks later, after the meeting during coffee time, Carol sidled up to me. "They have a meeting for you, too, you know, dear." Carol looked like a perfectly nice housewife from the Midwest. She favored sherbet-colored shirtdresses, smelled like Aqua Net, and her purse looked like a little picnic basket. I tried to picture her at the library, stashing vodka bottles on shelves behind self-help books.

"Oh, I don't have a drinking problem or anything." I gestured vaguely toward Mother.

"No, dear. Next time, go downstairs to the Alateen meeting. It might help." I had seen the sign in the hallway for a few weeks now, with a big black arrow pointing ominously down the steep metal stairs.

During Mother's next meeting, I followed the arrow down to the basement. The hall was dark and I tried the lights, but they didn't work. Still, it wasn't difficult to locate the meeting—a kind of rumble emanated from the end of the corridor. It sounded like heavy furniture being moved around. I followed the ruckus until I stood in front of a door. This must be the place. I took a breath and walked in.

About ten young people my age were in various poses of dismay, rage, and despondency. Metal chairs were set in a circle, where one girl held her head in her hands sobbing uncontrollably, while another boy stood on a chair and shouted obscenities at the ceiling. One boy just sat and stared straight ahead. Another young woman was lying on the floor with her arms shielding her face. A middle-aged man wearing an adhesive name tag that read SID was trying to calm a kid who was jumping up and down screaming, "No," over and over. It was so loud no one had noticed me come in.

"Okay, people, let's settle in the circle," Sid boomed over the din, placing a large hand on the "no" boy's shoulder. Everyone stopped what they were doing and sat down. I joined the circle.

"So who'd like to start? Anyone? I see we have someone new here today." Everyone turned and looked at me. I stared down at my lap.

"There's no pressure to speak, so don't worry." Sid was wearing a short-sleeved, white, button-down shirt and a tie. He was dark and burly with black tufts of hair on his arms.

"I'll start," the loud boy said.

"Great. Thanks, Rich." Sid crossed his arms and hunkered down in his folding chair. All the kids copied him, so I did, too.

"Well, I think I told you last time I was going to spend the weekend at my mom's while my dad went on a business trip."

"Yes, Rich, and how did that go?"

"Not so hot. So, Friday after school when I walked in the door, my mom was already totally out of it on the couch, and I had a friend with me and he saw her. And her dress was all hiked up and stuff."

"And how did that make you feel?"

I sat in the room and listened to them talk about their parents' drinking problems. There was a lot of sorrow and pain, but at the same time, I didn't hear anyone saying anything I could relate to. None of it sounded like what went on in my house. It was ... Dad had too many highballs and forgot my birthday, or Mom fell asleep on the couch. Well, none of that sounded like ... my mom tried to run me over, or my mom was arrested at my sister's high school graduation and was dragged off screaming in her blue nightie. Where was the support group for that? My mother drank and she became someone else, but she was also nuts. I left the meeting feeling confused and as if I didn't belong there. I didn't seem to belong anywhere. Except maybe the theater.

In a weird art-imitating-life occurrence, I auditioned for and was cast in a production of Neil Simon's play *The Gingerbread Lady*. One day I had seen the poster announcing auditions in the student lounge of the liberal arts building. The little theater group was not affiliated with the school for the arts, so I figured the competition wouldn't be that fierce. I was right; the director called me that evening to offer me the part. The play was about a washed-up nightclub singer in her forties named Evy, who gets out of rehab and goes home to try to live her life sober. I played Evy's daughter, Polly, the spunky, resilient teenager who loves her mom and tries to help her get back on her feet. So I was basically playing myself, albeit the bittersweet, corny Neil Simon version of myself.

I loved being in a play again, and I was glad to spend my evenings at rehearsal, not sitting at the dinner table with Mother, trying to make chitchat over a pot roast while she chain-smoked. Sometimes I went from rehearsal to the radio station where Amy was answering phones for Oedipus, the hot DJ of the moment. From there, we'd go out dancing for a few hours and not get home until after the bars had closed and Mother was asleep.

After about a month of sobriety, Mother decided to run for the position of leader of her AA meeting. I actually made signs for her, using posterboard and markers. She won, using that charm that I knew so well and saw right through; I was no longer impressed by her talent for manipulation. During this uneventful time at home Mother went back to work on her book, got bathed and dressed each day, and even made a pot of coffee for me and Amy before we went off to school in the morning.

"Wendelson," said Amy, heading out with her steaming go-cup, "catch you later maybe at the station. Thanks for the coffee, Mrs. Rea."

"Have a wonderful day, girls," Mother exclaimed. It was almost like the old Donna Reed days in Connecticut.

My play opened and Mother attended the first performance. It seemed painfully obvious to me that I was playing a version of myself and that I was onstage with a character very much like Mother, except with more one-liners. During my big speech at the end of the play where my character cries, yells, and begs her mother to stop drinking, I felt that it was clear that I was speaking directly to her. But Mother didn't seem to see it, or didn't want to.

"Well," she said afterward, shrugging her mink-draped shoulders, "it's not one of his best plays, is it?"

Of course, the play had a happy ending. The Gingerbread Lady goes on a bender and hits rock bottom again after being beaten by her lover. Then her friends (the Gingerbread Lady had two—two more than Mother) and her daughter gather around her, and she sees that she's hurt herself and the people she loves, and everyone forgives her, and she stops drinking, and it ends with everyone happy and hugging and joking.

A week into the run, I got home from performing the show to find Mother sitting in a living room armchair in the dark. I knew she was there because I could see the little orange point of her cigarette.

"Mother?" I switched on the lights. She was staring straight ahead. She was wearing the blue nightgown. *Oh, shit*, I thought.

"I just got off the phone with Carol." It was eleven o'clock at night, which struck me as a bit late for a chat with her sponsor.

"Is everything all right?" I had that old feeling, my stomach instantly in knots.

"I told her I was resigning my position as leader of the meeting."

"Why?"

"It's Carol!" Mother rose from the chair and started pacing back and forth like a caged animal. "She hates me! I swear she's trying to drive me to drink. That's what she wants!"

I pointed out to Mother that just couldn't be true. Carol was her sponsor after all and only wanted to support her.

"She's jealous of me. Now that I'm group leader, she's gaslighting me!"

It was hard for me to imagine Carol as Charles Boyer's evil character in the movie *Gaslight*, trying to drive his wealthy but fragile wife (Ingrid Bergman) insane. I had also never heard *gaslight* used as a verb. I resisted a temptation to run over to the light switch and flick it on and off—something Boyer does to push his wife over the edge. Of course, there was no need; Mother was already there.

"Come on, Mother." I was really tired and I had classes in the morning, which I would probably be late to.

"Carol is the ringleader and she's turned them all against

me. Of course she's jealous of my brains, my beauty. She's a fucking librarian!"

"It's late, Mother, maybe you should—"

"I'm simply better than any of them and they can't stand it!"

"Please, Mother, try to calm down."

"I'm not going back. Ever." She marched past me, then stopped at the bottom of the stairs. "Never screw a spider," she announced to no one in particular.

Her paranoia didn't surprise me; I wondered why it hadn't happened sooner. I chalked it up to another failure on my part. Mother's turn at AA had lasted three months. Life was not a Neil Simon play. Why didn't I know that by now?

The night the play closed, I came home late after the cast party. As I passed the bathroom on my way to my bedroom, I heard Amy's voice. It was hard to hear, as Mother had her TV blasting.

"Wendelson? Is that you?"

"Yeah," I spoke to her through the door.

"Can you get me outta here? I've been in here since three o'clock this afternoon." It was now midnight.

I tried the door, which opened easily with a little jiggling.

"Omigod, thank you!" Amy was wearing a T-shirt and panties.

"Jesus, you mean you've been in there for nine hours?"

"Yeah, I came in to take a shower and then I couldn't

open the door. I banged, I screamed. Nothing." Mother's bedroom door was just diagonally across the way. Clearly, she had been too out of it to hear.

"I'm so sorry."

"It's not your fault. I mean, I was too afraid to jump out the window. So I shaved my legs, I did my nails, I took a nap, you know."

"I can't believe my mom didn't hear you," I lied.

"Must be the TV. It's superloud."

I nodded.

"Hey, I'm late for work. Wanna come to the station with me?"

"No, thanks. I'm going to sleep. How about tomorrow?"

"Sure, Wendell. I gotta get dressed."

I went to my room and got ready for bed. I heard Amy bustling around, then the front door closing and her Camaro driving away. The play was done, and I was finishing up the semester with one B, two C's, and a D in my costume class—I hadn't studied for the final because I just didn't care. It was easier to be a ghostlike presence in my own life, sleepwalking through the days.

The next night, I went to the station with Amy. The story of Amy's being locked in the bathroom for nine hours had been on the WBCN news all that day. Amy had been enjoying her celebrity status, and when I got to the station, people asked me, "Oh, are you the one with the mom who couldn't hear Amy screaming and beating on the door for nine hours?" Yes, it was my mom, my bathroom.

Oedipus was in the booth doing his show, and Amy was answering the phone and taking requests. I watched Oedipus talking into the microphone, coolly flipping buttons on the board in front of him. He was a mystery—no one knew his real name, where he came from, how old he was. Nothing. He had this iceman persona that I could feel through the thick glass separating him from the rest of us ordinary people. There was nothing special about his looks. He was not handsome or tall; kind of scrawny—the kind of guy you'd walk past without noticing except that his hair was dyed hot pink. He probably got beat up every day in high school, but now he was Oedipus, the world's first punk-rock DJ. Sometimes he'd flash a reptilian smile at us through the glass, a smile that said he had the power and we were still little girls.

I was uneasily returning one of these smiles when a group of young men burst out of the elevator into the room, swearing in thick North London accents. Their manager, a middle-aged, fluffy-haired, portly type in a tight checked suit, introduced himself to us and said that the band had an interview on the air. They had been playing gigs in town, and he had brought copies of their record to the station. One of the boys stood out, to me anyway, as he seemed quieter than the rest and wasn't quite as drunk. He was not much taller than me, with cropped dark hair, pale skin, and incredibly sweet brown eyes. He was wearing jeans and a white T-shirt that said FUCK ART LET'S DANCE, and lace-up Doc Martens boots. We looked at each other, and it seemed to me that we had met somewhere before, but that was impossible of course. He smiled at me like he knew my secret.

The manager, whose name was Kellogg, puffed himself up and, making a sweeping arm gesture, said, "This is Madness. These are my boys." They all piled into the studio boisterously to be interviewed, all seven of them. I just kept looking at the one, and he at me. All the boys took turns at the microphone, and I heard him say his name was Lee and he played saxophone in the band. It was their first time in the States, and they were going down to New York tomorrow to play some more shows before touring the Midwest.

After the interview, they all spilled out of the booth.

Lee walked up to me.

"What's your name?" He had soft eyes like I remembered my dad having.

"Wendy."

"Like in *Peter Pan?*" He chuckled.

"Yeah, like in *Peter Pan.*"

"Can you fly then? You look like an angel, ya know."

I told him I couldn't fly and I wasn't an angel.

"You coming back to the hotel?" He was carrying his sax case. He lit up a Kent.

"Um, sure." I had heard Kellogg saying he was going to pick up some more records to drop off at the station.

"You got a car?"

A few minutes later, we were in my car driving down Boylston Street to Lee's hotel. Amy had Kellogg jammed in her Camaro with a few of the other boys in the band in the backseat, and a taxi took the rest.

The hotel was really a motel and a dump. We sat on the bed in Lee's room, surrounded by all the other guys and beer cans, and talked. He told me he'd basically started playing the sax because it was either that or a life of crime. He had already been sent to a reformatory for breaking into parking meters, and his dad had died in jail. He told me he had a girlfriend back in England and he'd known her since they were kids. He took my hand and said he wanted to ask me something.

"What is it?"

"Can I come home with you?"

I told him sure, trying to be cool and not show how wildly thrilled I was that he had asked, and he got his suitcase and his sax. We managed to leave without anyone's noticing us; they were all too busy getting hammered. I saw Amy talking to Kellogg and figured she was a big girl and could take care of herself.

We drove down Storrow Drive along the Charles toward Belmont. We rolled down the windows and Lee fiddled with the radio, finding some Stan Getz on a jazz station. The wind whipped around us and the music played and I wondered if I was about to have my first groupie experience. Then Lee told me he didn't want me to get the wrong idea. He was tired of hotels, and the rest of the lads would be up all night partying and he just wanted some peace and quiet. He wanted to get some sleep. I was a bit disappointed that he wasn't going to try anything. I was quiet for a time and then he said, "Besides, I couldn't do that to you. I'm going far away and who knows what'll happen."

When we got to my house, it was two in the morning and all the lights were out. Since my relationship with this man was doomed to innocence, I didn't think twice about bringing him home; it was my house, too, and I was twenty years old. I took Lee into the guest room on the first floor. He pulled back the covers, lay down, and fell asleep immediately. His saxophone was parked in the corner in a case. I went upstairs and tried to sleep.

I woke up to find Mother standing over me, glaring at me like a cobra before the strike.

"Who the hell is that?" she hissed, making her eyes all schrinchy as a cloud of cigarette smoke filled my small, dark room.

"Oh . . . ," I stammered. I had forgotten about the sleeping sax player in the guest room. "That's just a friend, he's just sleeping in the guest room so he can get some, um, sleep." I explained that he was a musician and that I had met him last night and offered him a quiet place to sleep for the night. The quiet part was quickly coming to an end I could see.

"It's that girl with her fucking rock 'n' roll lifestyle!" she shouted. "You fucked him in my house!" Her voice kept getting louder.

For a brief moment, I pondered the irony of this accusation. How many times had I woken up to an unidentified, furry-backed sleeping mound in our guest room, or a complete stranger at the breakfast table? Guys named Ted, Norman, Roger, Dick. Men in tailored suits with silk ties and cuff links, or blazers and Gucci loafers, or the one in the flannel shirt who drove a pickup truck and kept his conversation to single syllables. I couldn't even remember what he looked like, let alone his name. And yet, here was a man with whom I had not had sex and that was a big problem for her.

I denied that anything had happened between us in the house, and she didn't believe me and told me to get him out. She had apparently talked to him, because she made some snobby reference to his accent, which was working-class Camden Town. I actually think that this was what bothered her the most. If I had brought home someone wearing an ascot with a posh accent, she would have brought him breakfast in bed on a tray.

I dressed quickly and crept downstairs to find Lee, looking sleepy but perfectly content sitting on the end of the bed.

"I think your mum doesn't like me." He yawned and scratched his head and smiled. "I suppose she has someone special and she knows it."

It was sweet that he viewed my mother's lunacy as loving protection. I thought about this for a second, then realized that his saxophone case was missing from the room, gone from the corner it had been in last night. Mother had obviously taken it, probably sneaking in when Lee was asleep or in the bathroom.

Lee was expected back at his hotel within the hour, as they were all heading down to New York to continue their tour. I raced through the house looking everywhere. Finally, we had to go or he would miss the band bus. We went through the garage to get to my car, and there on top of the woodpile was his sax. We grabbed it and I drove him back to the seedy motor court. I stood with him in the parking lot while the roadies loaded equipment into a big bus and the rest of the band straggled by in various stages of hangover.

"What did you two get up to last night then?" said Chris, the guitar player. "Up all night reading poetry?"

Everyone snickered.

"Why don't you come down to New York with us?" Lee took my hand and squeezed it.

"I really can't." I didn't see how, as I had school and crazy-mom patrol.

"I just want to talk to ya. Come on, please. I told ya, no funny business." A pop star with principles. I wanted to go with him; I ached to go. I wondered in a flash why I was so responsible. Who had made me this way? I wrote my phone number and address on a matchbook I found in my jacket pocket.

"Call me? Or write to me, okay?" I pushed it into his palm.

He tucked it in his pocket. "Yeah, I will. I'll call ya in a few days."

I gave him a kiss while the band hung out the windows whooping at us. The bus started up and the driver honked the horn. Lee got on, then stuck his head out the bus window and smiled at me until I couldn't see him anymore.

Amy moved out shortly after Lee's departure. She had found an apartment near Emerson. "You know, your mom blames me for your so-called trampy behavior."

I only wished I had had the opportunity to be a tramp. "Yeah, I know. Sorry about that."

Amy loaded her stuff, packed in milk crates, into the trunk of the Camaro. "No worries, Wendelson. I do have a rock 'n' roll lifestyle, and I love it." She threw her arms around me and gave me a big hug.

I watched her get into her car.

"And I don't give a shit what your mother thinks." She scrutinized me for a second, then added, "And you shouldn't either. See ya, girlfriend."

A week later, I got a big greeting card with red roses all over it postmarked from Detroit that said FOR MY WONDERFUL SWEETHEART. Lee wrote, telling me that he had tried to call me three times, but had talked to Mother, who wasn't very happy about it, especially when he had called once at two in the morning. Of course, she hadn't told me that he had called at all.

chapter fifteen

PUCK PANTS

I didn't so much drop out of Boston University; I just sort of stopped going. Somehow it seemed pointless marking time in school when I could just get a job and be paid for it. I started working at Out of Town News, a big international newsstand in the middle of Harvard Square. I froze my butt off that winter, standing outside taking change for newspapers and magazines. As a job, it was a bit boring, but the people were nice and I liked being in Harvard Square. Sometimes I worked the cash register inside, where it was warmer, and called my sister in Missouri on the office phone when my boss wasn't around. She was doing well in school and thinking about a career in journalism. I was glad someone in our family had direction. It certainly wasn't me.

At the newsstand, I also got to look at all the British fashion and music magazines. I would scan the latter for news of Lee. Things were going well for Madness. They were starring on *Top of the Pops* and playing to packed houses.

One day in the spring I was at work when I overheard two people talking about a new theater that was going to be starting up at Harvard. It was going to be run by Robert Brustein, who had previously run the graduate theater program at the Yale School of Drama. He was bringing a lot of people from Yale to Harvard, and the buzz was big. The Loeb was just a few blocks away on Brattle Street, so on my lunch hour I walked over. I went through the glass doors into the theater lobby and spied a tall, brown-haired man dressed in black, rumpled clothing. He was in his late twenties and looked as if he hadn't bathed in a while. He was wearing a tool belt with lots of rolls of different-colored tape hanging on it, and he was swearing and loading batteries into a flashlight.

I smiled at him, trying to look both cute and capable. "Hi. Um, I was wondering if I could apply for a job here at the theater."

He kept fiddling with the flashlight. "Piece of shit," he muttered under his breath at the flashlight.

"I heard they were looking for people."

He looked up at me. "You have any tech experience?" He snapped the top on the flashlight and tossed it into a big, black wooden box at his feet.

"Not really, no." I was too embarrassed to tell him I had once run the light board in high school.

"Great. You're hired. Come back at noon on Saturday."

"Wow, really? That's fantastic! Thanks."

"Sure. When you come back, ask for me, my name's Randy. I'm the technical director."

"Okay, Randy. And thanks again!" I resisted the temptation to kiss his hand and skipped out of the theater amazed at my luck. Here was a chance to work in the theater behind the scenes, an opportunity to listen and learn and be around talented people. I would have taken a job cleaning the toilets if they had asked me.

I immediately gave my notice at the newsstand, excitedly telling everyone there about my new job at the American Repertory Theater, as it was to be called. I reported for work and Randy put me on the scenery crew with four other pretty young women who were all around my size and all blond. We were like Randy's harem stage crew or something.

We were responsible for moving huge pieces of scenery onstage to transform a child's playground, where the first act took place, into a prewar apartment on the Upper West Side of New York, for the second act. All this was to take place during the fifteen-minute intermission for a new play called *Terry by Terry* that was opening the season. It was to be in repertory with *A Midsummer Night's Dream*. We dragged the towering walls of built-in bookshelves and windows by ropes. The set actually had a ceiling, which, once we had locked the walls to each other, had to be lowered with pulleys from above the stage. The first time we did the change, it took forty-five minutes and we were all crying by the end of it. Randy seemed to relish his role as slave master. All he needed was a whip.

"Okay, girls, let's try it again!" Randy boomed.

This required putting the set back to its original position and then repeating the change. By the end of that first day, the guy who had designed the set, some Yalie named Andrew Jackness, had been dubbed by his short, blond, non-weight-lifting crew "Jackass." Jackass sat in the theater eating a sandwich while we groaned, pushing and pulling the set back into place. Randy licked his lips and seemed to get off even more the sweatier we became.

"Jesus, Randy," said a girl named Lisa, who was mopping her brow with the bottom of her T-shirt. Another girl, Linda, started to cry harder.

"I said one more time! We need to get this sucker down to fifteen minutes, tops!" Randy hollered at us, brandishing his stopwatch. Jackass broke open a bag of Lay's potato chips and propped his feet up on the chair in front of him. I imagined him being drawn and quartered in Harvard Square.

Even though every day of my new job was like reporting for duty on a slave ship and having to row for twelve hours, it was still the theater and I never missed my old job making change at the newsstand. Our crew worked hard all during technical rehearsals until, on opening night, we had finally got the change down to half an hour. Only then, with a full house waiting for the second act to begin and the stage manager and the house manager backstage arguing with Randy, did Randy see the error of his ways. It wasn't really our faults: Jackass had designed the Moby-Dick of sets. It was enormous and took up the entire stage. And the play sucked.

The next day, Randy went out trawling on Brattle Street for beefy men to join his set crew, and we little women were relocated to different departments. Granted a reprieve, I was given a job in wardrobe that even came with a small raise. With this extra money, I was able to finish paying off my gargantuan therapy bill to Dr. Keylor.

I loved my new job as a wardrobe assistant, even though I knew almost nothing about sewing. My boss was a hilarious gay guy named Don Swanson. He was a little, puckish man with a raunchy sense of humor and a laugh that sounded like the Wicked Witch's. He chain-smoked Kools and had one of those beards that made him look like a beatnik version of Satan. Soon we were best friends, and he didn't care that I didn't know how to sew or fix wigs. "Oh, just beat it with a stick!" he would cackle.

My duties included doing the laundry for all the actors and actresses, any repair work that needed to be done, and helping with quick changes backstage. I had to sew up holes in Carmen De Lavallade's bodysuit that she wore as Titania and strap Mark Linn-Baker into his flying harness for Puck, then test it by standing on a chair and trying to lift him. After the show, I fluffed the white, furry trousers he wore as Puck with a wire hairbrush. I held a flashlight in my teeth and helped the lovers change backstage for the wedding scene. And I watched the play—every night. The onstage chorus, dressed in iridescent green robes, sang music from

The Fairy-Queen by Purcell. It was a wonderful production of the play—comical and well acted, with touches of sadness and darkness, too. I loved just being at the theater, the way it smelled, looked, and made me feel. Watching the shows from the wings every night, I felt that I was home.

I liked to deliver the laundry to the men's dressing room, which was more lively and less serious than the women's. The actresses seemed more interested in their preparation, whereas the men's idea of a warm-up was to have a cigarette and read the paper. It reminded me of going backstage to see my dad at the Guthrie when I was a little girl. He'd be in his dressing room after the play in his undershirt taking off his makeup and having a beer. Which probably explains why I had innocent crushes on all those guys at the A.R.T.

During rehearsals for *Midsummer Night's Dream*, I had started talking with an actor in the cast. We were both backstage—he was waiting for his next entrance, and I was waiting for my next costume change. He was playing one of the fairies and wore a green bodysuit that covered all of him, including his face. It was like talking to a giant stalk of celery.

He and I whispered backstage about the play and about Boston; he was from New York. His name was Michael, and he was very funny and seemed nice, even though I couldn't tell what he looked like because of the bodysuit. After a week or two, he asked me out for coffee between shows on Saturday. No one had ever asked me out for coffee; it sounded very intellectual, very New York. I imagined dark-wood-paneled rooms in Greenwich Village, filled with poets and people strumming guitars. I immediately said yes.

I told him I'd meet him outside the stage door, after I'd picked up the laundry. I ran through the dressing rooms, picking up damp socks and T-shirts off the floor. I hurled them at Don and asked him to put them in the wash.

"I have a date," I said.

"Bitch. Jesus, I hope it's not with one of the actors. Find out if he's married!" Don yelled after me.

I ran out the stage door and looked around. People were milling about, waiting or talking. I looked around for Michael. Then I noticed a man standing by himself in jeans and a leather jacket. He was handsome and had a Roman nose. His hair was black and curly and he looked happy to see me. I felt as if we were meeting for the first time, and I suddenly felt quite shy. It had been easier to talk to him when I couldn't see his face and it was dark. But now I could see he was a man and, as it turned out, ten years older than me—ancient, thirty. We went down the street to this coffee place in a basement, and he did most of the talking. I felt in awe of him; he was witty and smart and very sure of himself. I learned that Michael was a New Yorker and Jewish. His parents had divorced; his mother was dead. I said I was sorry about his mother. I didn't tell him I wished my mother were dead.

"What about you?"

"Oh, I'm just trying to figure out what I want to do with my life." I shrugged, suddenly feeling really insipid, like Gidget or something.

"And what's that?" He smiled and looked at me.

"I guess I'm not sure." I explained how I had dropped out of college, had worked at a newsstand, and was now working at the theater and liked my job. Talking to him made me realize that I couldn't talk about my plans or dreams because I didn't have any. I was amorphous. I had no idea who I was, what I liked or disliked. I had spent so much time as Mother's warden, and Robbie's bodyguard, that I had subjugated a large part of myself that was, from lack of tending, small and undeveloped. When I walked into a grocery store, I would walk up and down the aisles, like a robot, aimlessly looking at all the boxes and jars wondering what I should buy. Did I like green beans? Cheerios? Cheddar cheese? I didn't know. Living my little half-life, I was so used to not thinking for or of myself. I was just going along. Just existing.

On opening night of *Midsummer* there was to be a big party, a splashy affair, in the theater lobby after the show. The high society of Boston would be there, in addition to all the critics from New York, and the entire cast and crew. Michael would be there.

"What are you going to wear, darling?" inquired Don. I hadn't the faintest. For the last week, all the crew members had been in technical and full-dress rehearsals, which, for everyone but the actors (who had Equity contracts and had to be given time off), had been virtually all day and all night. There was always mending to do,

Puck pants to fluff, boots to shine, wigs to spray, wash to do. The theater was like a factory that was open twenty-four hours a day. I'd been crashing on the ironing board. I couldn't remember the last time I had seen the sun or changed my clothes.

"This?" I said, gesturing to my jeans and ratty T-shirt.

"No, Cinderella, you will not go to the ball in *that*." Don raised his hand and shook a set of keys, looking like a gay jailer. The keys were to the private costume collection that was kept locked in a room above the stage. I followed him up the stairs and he opened the door.

"Now let's see, kiddo." He disappeared into the racks of clothes. "What color are your eyes?"

"They're blue."

Don picked out a midnight-blue sheath dress with netting on the arms and across the back. "Try this on. It's from the forties, which I think will be a good decade for you."

I went behind a rack to put on the dress. It fit me perfectly. Don tossed some pumps over to me. I came out from behind the rack and took a few turns up and down the room, modeling for him.

"Not bad. Dramatic but not too pushy. Very Veronica Lake." He stood looking at me with his arms crossed and a hip jutting out.

"What are you going to wear?"

"Jesus, you must be kidding. This old queen is going home to his bottle of Kahlúa." He turned and I followed him out into the hallway.

"But you're my date."

"You wouldn't catch me dead at one of those parties."

I thanked him for stealing something for me to wear.

"Anytime, princess. Now, have fun and don't turn into a pumpkin," he quipped, and was gone.

The party was in full swing by the time I got there. I was disappointed to see Michael talking to the actress who played Hippolyta. She was a Nordic-blonde type, pretty and tall, your basic queen of the Valkyries. I wondered what kind of girls he liked. He looked all lit up; he was talking animatedly to the actress. His dark hair was a little wet from his having washed his face, and it tumbled across his forehead, making him look even more dashing than usual. *Oh well*, I thought, *what a waste of a beautiful dress*. Maybe I could have a drink and sneak out.

I walked over to the bar, trying not to wipe out in my heels on the waxed wooden floor. I hadn't had much practice with the standard trappings of womanhood: high heels, makeup, panty hose, perfume. I actually tried to avoid them because they seemed like things my mother used to entice men. Makeup seemed like a trick, a way of attracting attention that was fake and predatory. Even standing there all dressed up made me feel like an impostor. I was pretending to be a woman. Pretending to be sexy.

Suddenly Michael was there behind me when I turned with my glass of champagne.

"I see you have legs." He laughed. Everyone at the theater, if they had noticed me at all, had only seen me in my work clothes—black pants and shirt.

"Yes, there they are. My legs." I felt once again like a dumb bunny.

"So you *are* a girl." He led me out onto the dance floor.

"I guess so." His arm embraced my waist.

"But it seems a reluctant one." He smiled at me and I had to look away because his face was so close to mine. We danced to a few songs, then he lured me into the costume shop, where we made out on one of the cutting tables. I went home with him that night.

I started spending a lot of time at Michael's apartment. I still felt a bit shy around him; he was older and seemed to know much more than I did. He had friends come and visit from New York. They were all sophisticated and up on current events. We would go out for drinks after the show, and everyone would be laughing and talking about so-and-so's new book or the presidential primaries. I felt so dull next to his New York friends. I just couldn't imagine what he saw in someone like me.

When he started to ask me what really interested me, I said the theater, books, movies, art. He asked me if I had ever considered taking photographs. He thought I would be good at it. He encouraged me to start taking pictures and even took me out and bought me a camera. I took photographs of lots of stuff—the actors, diners, trees, barns. I decided to apply to film school in New York. I had loved my film classes at BU, so maybe I would love film school. On the application you could either submit a film or photographs you had taken. I sent in my pictures, thinking I didn't have a chance in hell.

At Michael's apartment one morning while he was in the shower, I was snooping around and found some letters from a woman on his desk. I didn't open them; I was too afraid he might catch me and of what the letters might say. I felt a horrible sense of dread all day.

That evening after the show we were having a drink at a bar down the street and I asked him about the letters, feeling sick. "Who are they from?"

"They're from my girlfriend." He acted as if it didn't matter that he was telling me now that he had a girlfriend.

"You have a girlfriend?"

"Yeah, actually she's coming up to visit me this weekend."

"I thought I was your girlfriend," I said. I felt like I was going to barf.

"Well, Wendy, this is fun and everything, but you're twenty years old and I'm not interested in anything serious—"

His speech was interrupted by my drink flying into his face from across the table.

I stood up while he wiped his face with a cocktail napkin. He was smiling slightly, looking embarrassed. People were staring at us and my hands were shaking.

"If she comes up here, I don't want to see you again." I stormed off.

The next day at work, I saw Michael as usual backstage but didn't look at him or speak to him. I felt miserable—jealous of this other woman and foolish for throwing the drink at him. I was acting like my mother, and look where it had got me. He probably hated me now.

Michael was waiting for me after I came out the stage door. "Can I talk to you?" He didn't seem mad.

My face burned and I could barely bring myself to look at him. "I'm sorry I threw the drink at you. I was so angry," I stammered.

"It's okay," he said, half smiling. "I have to say I wasn't expecting it."

We started to walk down the street together. It was drizzling lightly and the streetlights shone on the trees that lined Brattle Street. The air smelled like lilacs.

"I won't let her come," he said. "She's not even really my girlfriend. I just said that because I was afraid."

I looked down at the sidewalk, which was all shiny with the rain. "What are you afraid of?" I didn't understand.

"I'm afraid of you," he said quietly.

When we reached his apartment, his message machine was blinking. I dropped my stuff on the couch while he went over and pressed the flashing button. It was my mother's voice on the machine. She cleared her throat theatrically and then spoke. It was chilling to hear her in Michael's apartment, where I thought I was safe.

"Hello. I wanted Wendy to know that the FBI just called me and informed me that her sister, Robin, has committed suicide." Then she hung up.

"Oh my God. Who the hell was that?" Michael started

to rewind the machine. He played the message again. I told him it was my mother. He stared at me for a second with his mouth hanging open. "What should we do?" he asked, sounding panicked.

"Nothing." I picked up the phone and called Robin's dorm-room number. She answered and I asked her if she was okay.

"Yeah, I'm fine except you woke me up," she said, sounding cranky.

"Sorry, go back to sleep. I'll call back later in the week." I put down the receiver.

"So, your sister's fine? Is this some kind of a joke?"

"Not a joke exactly, but I'm sure Mother's having fun."

"But how did she get this number?"

"She probably called the theater and said it was an emergency," I said matter-of-factly. Then I gave him the short version of my struggles with Mother. He just listened and didn't say anything for a while.

"So why didn't you tell me any of this? I mean, this is pretty huge, having to handle something . . . someone like this." He searched my face, looking perplexed.

My throat felt all tight as I tried to explain. "Most people don't stick around when my mother makes an appearance. I guess I was afraid you'd disappear, too."

"Well, I'm not going anywhere, but I do need a drink."

We went to the kitchen and sat down at the little dinette table. He poured himself a scotch from a bottle he kept on top of the fridge. He poured me a small one and dropped a few ice cubes into it.

"Thanks." I sipped the burning flavor.

He sat down across from me, stirring his drink with his finger. "You know, you can't live your life for anyone else." He picked up the salt shaker. "You see, this is your mother." He placed it at one end of the table. Then he picked up the pepper. "And this is you." He put the pepper down at the other end. "She doesn't have any power over you really. You've given her that power."

"Me?" I eyed the salt shaker. "Well, first of all, that's wrong because she would be the pepper."

"Yeah, okay, I get it. It matches her black soul. You can be the salt." He switched the shakers on the table.

"That's more like it."

"And pretend the salt has a shit raincoat on."

"What are you talking about?"

"A shit raincoat that protects you from all the crap that she slings at you. She throws her insane garbage at you and it hits the shit raincoat and it falls off."

"I wish."

"The shit raincoat takes practice." He laughed, and it occurred to me that he hadn't run away yet.

I sort of saw what he was talking about. Not that I was a salt shaker, but that Mother was a separate entity, and a small and inconsequential one at that. She only loomed large in my mind; in reality she was an empty, sad wreck of a person. After spending more time talking to Michael, I began to realize that I had to make a break for freedom or she might just take me down the rabbit hole with her.

One day I was sitting in the wardrobe room with Don, reading the program for the theater's season, and I noticed that one of the actors, Max Wright, had worked at the Guthrie in Minneapolis, where my father had been for so many years. My face started to tingle and I felt a little queasy. Maybe he could tell me something about my dad.

I hadn't seen or heard from my father in ten years. Mother had told Robin and me that he had abandoned us for his new family all those years ago. As a ten-year-old girl, I had accepted this as the truth. Why had he found it so easy to walk away from his children? Why had he never even sent a letter or a postcard in ten years? I didn't have a photograph of him, but Mother told me I looked just like him. If he saw me on the street, would he recognize me?

"You should go ask Max," Don said. "It's your father, for Christ's sake."

A few weeks went by and I still couldn't muster the nerve to talk to Max about my father. Before the show, he was always at his dressing table in the corner, reading some heavy book about Brecht or Sartre, and I couldn't ask him there because so many people were around. After the show, he was always the first one to bolt out the door as soon as he had changed. I knew he was leaving soon to go back to New York, so there wasn't much time left.

"You better hurry up," Don warned, hands on hips and arching his eyebrows for emphasis.

The next night during the show, I was crossing through the theater lobby with some laundry and there was Max having a cigarette. This might be my last chance. I walked up to him and blurted out that I was wondering if he had met an actor named James Lawless at the Guthrie.

"Sure, I know Jimmy Lawless." He nodded.

I swallowed. "What's he like?"

"He's a really nice guy. Why are you asking?" Poor Max looked at me like I was one of those freaky autograph hounds who stalked the stage door.

"Well . . . he's my father and—"

"Jesus, you're Jimmy's kid! Omigod, how old are you?"

"I'm twenty."

"Christ, that makes me feel old."

"Um . . ." I was about to launch into my tale of woe when Max's head twitched up toward the monitor.

"Holy shit, that's my cue!" Max stubbed out his cigarette and ran like hell.

A nice guy. It wasn't much to go on, but Max hadn't said he was a monster with two heads. I sleepwalked back to the wardrobe room, where Don was sitting sewing, his mouth full of pins.

He saw my face and almost spit the pins out. "Omigod, you asked him, didn't you?"

I nodded and smiled.

He took a piece of paper out of his jeans pocket. "I took the liberty of getting the number from directory assistance."

He gave me the paper and handed me a roll of quarters. "Are you gonna be okay? Are you scared?"

"No, I'm not scared at all."

The truth was that I felt strangely calm. Suddenly I knew that this was the right thing for me to do, that I had to do it. It had just taken me some time to know it. Ten years.

chapter sixteen

THE FRIENDLY SKIES

This time on the airplane to Minneapolis, rather than getting wings from the flight attendant like the last time I made this trip, I ordered a Bloody Mary to calm my nerves. I had always been afraid to fly, and as the plane hurtled toward its destination, I looked out the window and wondered if my fear was connected to all the tumult I used to experience on airplanes—the tears, the feeling of emptiness when you leave something behind that is still a part of you.

"Sure you don't want me to come with you?" Michael had driven me to the airport in Boston.

"I think I should go on my own. But thanks."

"God, wait till your mother reads that note." He laughed maniacally like Dr. Frankenstein when they asked him if he was mad.

I smiled. Since Mother was barricaded in her fortress, I had scribbled a note about where I was going and left it on the kitchen table. I kept playing the movie of her reaction to the note over and over in my head, for fun. I could see her stumble down the stairs into the kitchen, go to the fridge for a quart of ice cream, and on her way back to her room notice the note. She would pick it up, holding it close to her face trying to read it in the dim light. Then her eyes would bulge and she'd throw back her head and scream like the lady in the scary movie when she sees the monster for the first time.

"You should probably turn off your answering machine for a few days," I told Michael at the gate.

"Good idea. You'd better go."

I kissed him and got on the plane.

When I got off in Minneapolis, I looked around. I searched for a face I hadn't seen in ten years but felt sure I would know. Strangers walked by lugging strollers and backpacks as I scanned the crowd. Then I noticed, across from my gate, standing next to a large potted palm tree, a distinguished-looking older man. He had beautiful, wavy white hair and was nattily dressed in a navy blue, pinstripe suit with a maroon paisley tie. His black shoes were shiny and pointy. I started to walk toward him. He had a big Irish face and blue, misty eyes, and he was chewing gum. He looked remarkably like me. He was also wearing makeup and hair spray because he had just been shooting a commercial for Red Baron pizza. I walked over to him; he stood there smiling.

"Daddy?"

"Sweetheart! Ha-ha!" He opened his arms wide, laughing.

I could see the gum dancing around on his molars like a little musical peanut, and I hugged him, breathing in the smells of my dad, which were the same after all this time: Trident spearmint gum, hair spray, and Dunhill cologne. It was a great smell.

"Let's go to the bar and have a drink."

We bellied up to the bar and I ordered coffee, and he had a perfect manhattan on the rocks with an olive.

He told me that my stepmother was on a business trip, so we would have the next few days to ourselves. "She sends her love." He gestured to my hair. "What color is that?"

I had been dyeing my hair with henna so it was red. I told him that my hair had started turning white when I was around nineteen. I didn't want to say that I'd often thought that Mother had given me the prematurely gray hair with all her shenanigans. But now I knew it was inherited.

"It runs in our family. Your grandmother has it and my brother and sisters, too." He looked down into his drink. "I'm just so happy to see you." He shook his head and looked up at me with tears in his eyes. I was crying, too. It was weird—like looking into a mirror after not having seen yourself for such a long time. Here we were, father and daughter, lost and found, sitting in an airport bar.

We went down to baggage claim, where my bag was the only one remaining. Daddy carried it through the parking garage, and we got into his huge, black Buick LeSabre. Classical music played on the radio as we drove through Minneapolis, which I had not seen since my childhood. He drove me past the old house on Humboldt Avenue, where Robbie and I used to live with him in the summers, and around the park where he played tennis while we rode our bikes, and down Mount Curve Avenue with all the elegant mansions, where Robin and I lived briefly after our mother had left him for Pop. We swung past the Guthrie Theater, with its modern concrete-and-glass façade, where we had watched him in *Twelfth Night* and *The Tempest* and other plays, and by Seven Pools, where our babysitters used to take us swimming in the summer, and Dayton's, where Daddy used to take us to buy our summer play clothes.

Their home was one I had never seen—a lovely, old stone house with lots of windows and a big fireplace across from the front door. It reminded me of a house in a fairy tale, which of course it was in a way. The house was filled with things I didn't recognize. Every rug, every chair, and every book was new to me, and I was painfully struck by how I had missed so much time with him and that it had gone on without me. The photographs in the house were of my step-mother's children. They had grown up with my father, I had not. The only pictures of me and my sister were in a clear plastic photo cube, which I picked up off the mantelpiece. I turned the box over in my hand, looking at snapshots of two little blond girls. We were all grown up now.

Daddy lit the charcoal in the grill out on the back porch. We were having steak and Caesar salad. He told me these were the only two things he knew how to make. He told me that he had learned how to grill steak from my grandfather, my mother's father, when they lived in Kansas City. Never poke the meat and always let it rest for ten minutes after cooking. He opened a bottle of red wine, and I set the table.

After dinner, we went to sit on the front porch. It was late and we were both tired from the day.

"Is there anything you want to ask me?" Daddy said. He lit a thin cigar. It was dark out by now, the only light from a lamp inside the house. The stars had come out, and the air pulsed with the chirruping of many insects.

"Why didn't you come to get us?"

For my whole life there was another life that I had never lived but had always imagined. In my ghost life I had grown up as Wendy Lawless, my father's daughter in a big house in the Midwest with all my siblings. I lived a normal, almost boring life, never moved, and walked to school carrying a lunch box.

"Well, your mother made it so difficult when she took you away." He shook his head, looking down at the ashtray. The cigar smoke smelled heavy and sweet.

"What do you mean, took us away?"

"I just didn't know where you were for the first few years."

I was stunned.

He went on. "I came to New York to tell you and your sister that I was getting married. That really upset your mother."

I remembered when he had come to New York to tell us that he was marrying Sarah—that was the un-Christmas, when Mother took all our toys away.

"After I got back, she wouldn't let me talk to you girls. Sarah even wrote to your mother trying to smooth things over, but it just made it worse."

I remembered Mother's showing us Sarah's letter, a card with flowers on it. Mother shook it at us and said, "How dare she speak to me like that!"

"Then, it all seemed to blow over. I was so relieved. I sent two airplane tickets for you and Robin to come out to the wedding. We drove to Sioux Falls, which was the closest place we could get married, because we each had only one day off."

"Then what happened?" I couldn't believe I was hearing this for the first time at the age of twenty.

"We waited at the airport. You weren't on the flight from New York. We waited and you weren't on the next flight or the next."

Of course we never got off the plane in Sioux Falls. While my dad and his bride-to-be and my future stepsiblings waited for us at the airport, we were sailing out of New York harbor on the *QE2*. Mother had told us he didn't want us there and we had believed her.

"Finally, we just drove to the courthouse wondering what had happened to you."

The wedding took place as planned without us. After the ceremony, everyone went back to the Holiday Inn and sat around the empty swimming pool. It was May and still chilly there. I imagined my father in a suit, with a boutonniere pinned to his lapel, sitting in a plastic chair holding a drink, staring down at the leaves at the bottom of the drained pool.

"It was only later that I found out what had happened. She had actually cashed in the tickets and disappeared, taking you girls with her. I hired a private detective, who found out you were in England. When we found that out, my brother, your uncle Billy, started to formulate a plan to come and get you; to essentially kidnap you back and return you to the States."

"But you never came."

He looked down at his hands, shaking his head. "No, I decided we couldn't do that. I thought it would be better to wait. I sent birthday cards and Christmas presents." He looked at me and I shook my head because we never got them.

"I knew one day you'd come back. And here you are."

"Yes." I smiled at him in the dark, hiding the big hole in my heart.

I went to bed that night in my father's house for the first time since I had been a child. I could hear him humming in the hallway, going into his room, and turning on a radio. I dreamed of those summers I used to spend with him—riding my bike, swimming in our little kiddie pool in the backyard, sleeping in a double bed with my sister.

In the morning, we sat at the kitchen table and drank coffee. He had a box of photographs that we looked through. I didn't even have a picture of him, and I had seen few baby pictures of myself. There were pictures of me and Robbie with our cousins and grandparents in Canada; one of us, at ages two and three, bundled up in navy-blue jackets, sitting in a wagon in a driveway somewhere on a fall day; and at the bottom of the box, one from 1192 Park that last Christmas. We are sitting on my father's lap in an armchair in front of the Christmas tree, dressed in matching red velvet jumpsuits with frilly, white lace collars. We look like sad little candy canes.

Looking at the photos, I felt adrift. This entire part of my life had been taken away from me by Mother. It was she who had decided it wasn't important.

"Why did you marry her?" He must have loved her at some point.

"Your mother told me she was pregnant, and in those days you got married."

"Pregnant with me?"

"Uh, no." He told me that after they had got married, my mother claimed to have lost the baby, fishing it out of the toilet and burying the fetus in the backyard. It was the kind of lurid detail that I recognized as her trademark. "You came along a year later."

"Are you sorry you married her?"

"Then I wouldn't have you girls." He pointed to the box of photos and said, "I want you to have those."

My father drove me to the airport the next day. I will always think of him in an airport; that's where we said our hellos and good-byes. I kissed him and promised to call soon and to come visit again.

On the plane ride home, I thought about how I would never get the time I had lost with my father. Those ten years were over. It seemed that everyone had paid a high price for what had happened—except for the person who had caused it all. She had cheated all of us. We'd been kidnapped and never even knew it. We did have a father who loved us, who could have helped us, and Mother had deprived us of our one shot at happiness.

The taxi drove up the big hill to my house. I paid the driver and carried my suitcase up to the front door. I thought of all the times I had returned home, not knowing what I would find on the other side of the door, my stomach turning over with the key in the lock. I thought of all the times I wished I hadn't lived here at all. I opened the door and walked into the living room, where my mother sat, leafing through a magazine as if it were just any other day. I put my suitcase down. She looked up. She was actually dressed and wearing makeup. The house looked tidy. I wondered where the hidden camera was. Who was this show for? Me?

"Oh, hello. This came for you." She picked up a white envelope from the coffee table in front of her and handed it to me. I wondered if she'd steamed it open. It was from NYU. I opened it. It was an acceptance letter. I had gotten in. I was moving to New York.

"So, how's your father?" she asked casually.

I wasn't going to answer that question. Might as well cut to the chase. "I want you to know that he told me what you did. Ten years ago, you cashed in the airplane tickets and you took us away—you kidnapped us. And I want you to know that I can never forgive you for that."

For the first time, I had successfully set off a bomb in the living room. The silence hung in the air and the smoke cleared as I watched Mother mentally rifle through her bag of tricks, trying to decide how best to proceed. She was like a bad actress trying to remember her lines.

"He's lying to you. He just wants to hurt me," she replied as if it were all ridiculous. "He's still in love with me," she said haughtily.

Always with the "me," I thought. Was this the best she could do?

"Why would he lie?"

"Because I am the only woman he's ever really loved," she oozed, as if she were telling me that not just the Tarleton Twins were in love with her, but all the boys at the barbecue.

"After all this time? He doesn't have a reason." I felt calm. "And who could hurt you? You don't have any feelings." *Careful,* I thought.

"I'm sorry you feel that way, Wendy. I always did the best I could." Her hand fluttered up to her throat, where it fiddled with the collar of her blouse. She gazed out the window, stalling for time.

"Well, I think your best was pretty damn lousy." This remark put an end to the Scarlett O'Hara routine.

"Oh, you do, do you? I suppose you think raising two children alone is easy." She stood up, tossing the magazine on the couch, and drew herself up. I could tell that she thought she'd scare me if I thought she was about to blow me to hell with her fury. But I wasn't afraid of her anymore. She seemed small to me. Like the pepper shaker on Michael's kitchen table. I could see now that she was a big phony, hollow inside.

"Anyway, it doesn't matter because I got into film school in New York. That's where I'm going." I held up the letter. "And I'm changing my name back to my real name. To Lawless."

"Oh, Wendy." Suddenly she was trembling and tears were running down her cheeks. "I know that I've made some mistakes, and I'm sure you hate me now." Black mascara streams fell from her cheeks, staining her silk blouse. She looked all crumpled, like she'd been stepped on.

"I don't hate you, but I can't forgive you."

"I'm sorry if I hurt you and your sister. You girls were my whole life. Everything I did was for you."

This was a big fat lie, but it made me feel sorry for her all the same. She lacked the necessary equipment for the job of motherhood, which partly wasn't her fault. It was just . . . missing, buried somewhere, like the phantom dead baby in the backyard.

"There isn't anything else to say. I'm going to go." I picked up my suitcase and turned toward the door.

"Of course you are. Everybody leaves."

Or gets driven away, I thought.

"My whole life everybody's abandoned me: my mother, my father, your father, your stepfather, Robin, and now you."

The mountainous waves of self-pity left me unmoved. I reached the door and opened it, clutching my suitcase and the acceptance letter. "Good-bye, Mother," I said.

"I'm all alone. With no one, with nothing."

"I think you'll be fine, Mother. The thing about you is, you always land on your feet. Good-bye." I pushed through the screen door and started across the front lawn. I heard the screen whine and knew she was behind me.

"That's it? Just good-bye? See you sometime?"

I turned. "Yes, I guess so."

She opened her arms wide and low. "Can't I give you a good-bye kiss?"

I was approximately four yards from the road. "All right, Mother."

She walked up to me and embraced me. Many emotions coursed through me at that moment. She was my mother and I still wanted her to love me, wished that she could. In her arms, I felt hatred, fear, pity, guilt. But somehow, in that instant, they canceled each other out and I felt nothing. I gave her a small hug, then I pulled gently away from her and headed for the street.

She cleared her throat. "Oh, before you leave, there's just one thing."

I stopped and turned to look at her. "What's that?"

"The money." She lit up a cigarette.

"What money?"

"My money that you inherit from my father that right-fully belongs to me."

Then it hit me. The money was all that she wanted. Her last-minute apology, the tears, the hug—it was just the final gambit. I didn't matter to her. I was nothing but an extension of her, like an extra arm. I'd sign over my trust fund to her and then I'd finally be free. All I had to do was give her the money, the payoff for her rotten childhood and having been saddled with Robin and me, and soon I'd be so far away and she'd be out of my life. I stood there with my suitcase, watching her puff away while her eyes shriveled into slits. It was at that moment I saw my chance to hurt her as much as she had hurt me. As much as she had hurt everyone.

"I'm not giving you the money," I announced.

She looked at me with an expression of high dudgeon that, of course, I had seen about a million times.

"But it's mine. You said you'd sign it over to me when you turned twenty-one," she spluttered, her voice starting to quaver. For once, I had pulled the rug out from under her.

"I've changed my mind," I said.

Switching strategies, she followed me. The anger dropped out of her voice, which took on the throb of a movie heroine pleading for her life on the witness stand. "But you promised me. You said you'd give me the money."

I turned on the path and regarded her with steely eyes. "I lied. Good-bye, Mother." I started to walk back down the hill. I could walk into town and get a bus.

"You monster! I'll hire a lawyer! That money is mine! You'll never get away with this!"

Mother followed me screaming, but I never looked back.

"Don't bother trying to come home! Ever!" she fumed. "Go to New York! Go to your father!"

And I did.

postscript

My sister dropped out of college, cashed in what was left of her trust fund, and made an award-winning documentary about pilgrims to Elvis's home, Graceland. She later moved to New York, waitressed, put herself through Hunter College, managed restaurants, and now works as a freelance writer.

I dropped out of film school and returned to acting, performing on Broadway, off-Broadway, and in regional theater across the country, including at the Guthrie. I married a screenwriter and live in Los Angeles with our two children.

My father walked me down the aisle and gave me away on my wedding day. He held both my children in his arms. He passed away at the age of sixty-three, surrounded by his wife, children, and stepchildren.

My mother was found dead in her apartment in Concord, New Hampshire, by the fire department after she had failed to appear at a chemotherapy appointment. She had been dead for four days. Although she had been diagnosed with colon cancer the year before, she'd instructed those nearest her not to contact me. When I discovered that she had died, her body had been in the morgue unclaimed for over three weeks. She was sixty-seven.

The police report stated that she had died in bed, watching the History Channel in her nightgown. It was blue.

acknowledgments

Enormous heartfelt thanks to my agent, Robert Guinsler, who saw something and said so. His Herculean enthusiasm for and undaunted belief in my book made this all happen. I feel lucky to have found him.

I am most grateful to my editor, Tricia Boczkowski, who gently pushed me to ask hard questions of the story, and whose almost clairvoyant understanding and fabulous sense of humor often made me feel as if she were finishing my sentences. Thanks to Alexandra Lewis, for her smart, fresh perspective, and coolheaded, calm answers to my sometimes frantic pleas for help.

Thanks to Simon & Schuster and Gallery Books, especially Louise Burke, Jen Bergstrom, and Kara Cesare, for embracing the book and running with it. To Eric Rayman for helping me change the names of the not-so-innocent.

The Menocal family for their permission to use my mother's portrait, and to Lisa Litwack for the astonishing cover art she created.

To my first readers: Aviva Erlich, Sara Eckel, Nancy Woodruff, Elizabeth Thomas, Bill Madison, Katherine Heiny, Samantha Alderson, and Meghan Daum.

Mark Rotella, Paul Elie, Stephen Morrow, Samantha Peale, Stefan Fatsis, Sophia Nardin, George Scott, Lisa Lou Banes, and Kathryn Kranhold, who were early champions of the book, and encouraged and emboldened me by trying to help find a home for it.

To my dear friends Dee LaDuke, Mark Brown, and Bob Cesario, who appeared at the dawn of this process and never stopped believing in me.

Jenny Ott, my oldest and best friend, for her unconditional love, fabulous food, and a spare room in New York while I worked on the manuscript.

To my father-in-law and mother-in-law, George and Diane Kidd, who welcomed me into their family many years ago like a daughter, and who have been there for the difficult times when I needed help most of all. Ellen, Stephen, and Nancy Kidd for their loving support.

I am beholden to Mary and Allen Welch, for their help in locating my mother's body.

My children, Harry and Grace, for their love and patience, and for giving me the chance to have a happy childhood after all, by giving one to them. You two are my heart.

Most of all, I am deeply grateful to my amazing husband, David Kidd, who always believed I could write this book, even when I wasn't sure. His unwavering love, assistance, wisdom, and faith in me literally brought this book into being. I love him more than words can express, and I could not have done it without him.

This reading group guide for Chanel Bonfire includes an introduction, discussion questions, ideas for enhancing your book club, and a Q&A with author Wendy Lawless. The suggested questions are intended to help your reading group find new and interesting angles and topics for your discussion. We hope that these ideas will enrich your conversation and increase your enjoyment of the book.

INTRODUCTION

In this strikingly honest memoir, actress Wendy Lawless shares the often-heartbreaking story of her childhood with an alcoholic and suicidal mother—equal parts Holly Golightly and Mommie Dearest—and the extraordinary resilience that allowed her to rise above it all.

Topics and Questions for Discussion

1. Why do you suppose Wendy Lawless chose to open *Chanel Bonfire* with her mother's first suicide attempt? What does this scene reveal about Georgann, as well as about nine-year-old Wendy and her younger sister, Robin?

2. When Wendy and Robin were children, Georgann told them about her abusive upbringing in the form of a bedtime story. Did knowing about her traumatic past make you more sympathetic? Why or why not? Do you think Georgann had any redeeming qualities as a mother? How do you think Wendy and Robin would answer this question?

3. Why did Wendy decide to contact her father after not seeing him for a decade? Given the circumstances, do you think James Lawless gave up too easily on trying to be involved in his daughters' lives? Why or why not?

4. Refusing to speak to her daughters for extended periods of time was Georgann's "most effective tactic" (page 68). Why was this form of punishment even more devastating for Wendy than being spanked with a hairbrush or sent to bed without supper?

5. In what ways is role-playing a theme in *Chanel Bonfire*? What motivated Georgann to frequently reinvent herself? Why did her transformations typically coincide with a move to a new town or city?

6. Discuss Wendy and Robin's relationship and how it changed in their teen years. "Robin had fully evolved into the defiant

one" (page 138), says Wendy. What role did Wendy play in their sibling dynamic? Did their relationship remind you of any of your own personal relationships?

7. "I loved just being at the theater, the way it smelled, looked, and made me feel" (page 264), says Wendy. What did the theater and performing represent to Wendy? How much of her desire to act had to do with her father?

8. In hindsight, Wendy had misgivings about leaving Robin alone in the "Snake Pit" with their mother when she moved into the college dorm. Was she right or wrong to leave her sister alone with Georgann? Why did Wendy later decide to move back in with her mother? How did being in the house with Georgann affect her?

9. Dr. Keylor gave Wendy a list of symptoms for a clinical diagnosis called "Cluster B," which the therapist believed applied to Georgann. Why did having this information give Wendy a sense of relief and make her feel as if she has made an "amazing discovery" (page 166)?

10. Re-read the scene on page 273 where Michael offered advice to Wendy using salt and pepper shakers as props. How did he make her see her relationship with her mother in a different way?

11. Wendy's high school drama teacher, Mr. Valentine, suggested she audition for university acting programs. Who else offered encouragement to her throughout the years? Why did Pop continue to provide some financial and emotional support to Wendy and Robin even after his divorce from Georgann?

12. Wendy's college roommate, Julie, once asked if she had "ever tried just talking" to her mother. Before reading *Chanel Bonfire*, would you have been inclined to offer similar advice to someone in a situation like Wendy's? How about after reading this book?

13. What is your opinion of Wendy as a narrator and how she tells her story? Why do you think she was able to stay grounded in the midst of such a chaotic and frightening upbringing?

14. Why did you choose *Chanel Bonfire* for your book club discussion? What are your overall thoughts about the book? How does it compare to other memoirs your group has read?

ENHANCE YOUR BOOK CLUB

1   Wendy enjoys the camaraderie while she's working at Joyce Chen. Host your book club discussion at a Chinese restaurant, order takeout, or whip up your own Chinese food feast.

2. Put together a *Chanel Bonfire* sound track and play it as background music during your book club gathering. Songs mentioned in the memoir include "Allison" by Elvis Costello, "In My Life" by the Beatles, "That's the Way of the World" by Earth, Wind & Fire, and "Sweet and Innocent" by Donny Osmond. Be sure to include something by Elton John, who Wendy once tripped accidentally outside a concert venue.

3. If you enjoyed *Chanel Bonfire*, consider adding another memoir about trying childhoods to your discussion line-up, such as *The Glass Castle* by Jeannette Walls, *Love Child* by Allegra Huston, or *Daughter of the Ganges* by Asha Miro.

4. Test your memory. Have each member bring a childhood photograph to the meeting. Discuss how much or how little you remember about the time it was taken.

A CONVERSATION WITH WENDY LAWLESS

Why did you decide to write a book about your childhood experiences? Was there a "lightbulb moment" when you knew you wanted to share your story?

I had been telling the story anecdotally for years—to make people laugh, or to shock or entertain, or to somehow pay them back for the expensive meal they were buying me! And often, people would urge me to write it down, write a book, a memoir. But I was afraid. I knew the story was so much sadder and uglier than the jokes I had told about it. And honestly, there were parts of it I wasn't eager to relive. It's one thing to be glib and toss out a line like, "My mother tried to run me over with the car." It's something else to remember it in detail and the circumstances and the emotions and feelings from the actual event. So I didn't. I was acting full-time on the stage in New York and married and then had a baby. My life was busy and full and I didn't feel the need to go back.

Then, by the time my second child had come along, we were living in Los Angeles and I'd fallen out of love with acting, so I decided to stop, except for an occasional commercial, and be at home with the kids full-time. And while I didn't miss the business of acting I did miss having a creative outlet, so I started to write. People always say you should write what you know, so I looked around the playgrounds where I spent a lot of my time, mostly alone because all the other kids seemed to be there with their nannies, and I wrote about that. They were all just short pieces, essays, about my kids, and being a mom in Hollywood, and being a mom who was raised by a mom who was nuts.

And after writing and thinking about these things for a while, I realized I couldn't ignore the fact that everything I was doing, with my life and my kids, was to not be like my mother. I had thought that I'd completely severed that part of my life from this, the past from the present, but now I couldn't ignore the fact that it still had a profound effect on me. It was an epiphany of sorts, and it came to me while sitting at a stop sign, and I started writing *Chanel Bonfire* that day, in the car.

What would you like people who have not yet read *Chanel Bonfire* to know about the book?

That it's a horrible and horribly funny story of two girls, sisters, who survive the shipwreck of their childhood, without a road map or a how-to manual. And that it has a happy ending.

I don't think it ruins things to know that. The story is scary enough and perhaps, for some people, so close to home that I don't worry that knowing things turn out for some of us will hurt their reading experience. I hope that reading the book may help some people come to terms with their own childhoods or recognize that their survival is a triumph they can cherish. And for younger people who may be struggling in similar situations, there is a light at the end of the tunnel: they can make it. And someday even laugh about it.

Did you read other memoirs while you were writing your own? If so, which ones did you find particularly inspiring or memorable?

I re-read *Running with Scissors*, I love his bravery and honesty. He really puts himself out there, and you feel guilty laughing, but the book is so funny and dark at the same time. I found *The Glass Castle* deeply moving. The opening image of that book, where the author drives in a limo past her own mother dressed in rags, rummaging through a Dumpster, punched me in the stomach right away. That was always how I thought my mother would end up, on the streets.

Your sister is featured prominently in the book. What was her reaction to being portrayed in print?

At first, before I was finished, she was upset, and didn't understand why I was writing the book. But she did send me pictures and some of her memories, which were helpful because our mother destroyed almost all the pictures of our childhood and adolescence and actually cut us out of the ones she did keep.

When she did start reading the full manuscript, she emailed me along the way at the very beginning and told me how much she was liking it. But it was uncomfortable for her when she reached the scenes of big emotional events and had to view them from someone else's point of view. Everything wasn't exactly the way she had remembered it. In some cases I was able to make scenes better with details she provided. But it was still strange and disorienting for her to read about her own life through my eyes—to be a character in someone else's book. That's understandable, I think.

In the end, she told me she was glad I had written our story.

One of the most compelling aspects of the book is your honesty. Were you ever tempted to hold back on revealing certain details that were painful to dredge up or that you thought might portray you or your sister in a less-than-flattering light?

I actually did leave out some of the more gruesome details from my mother's childhood. There are certain things she told me (when I was way too young to hear them, of course!) that will probably haunt me forever. I omitted them because I didn't want the book to be too dark, or miserable. Other than that, no, I didn't leave anything out. I really believe that the truth can't hurt you, because it's the truth.

Why did you decide on *Chanel Bonfire* as the title? How does it reflect the book? Were any other titles ever considered?

The title was originally just a chapter heading in the London section of the book, where the wild, teenage, backyard bonfire party scene was. My husband (the screenwriter David Kidd) and I were brainstorming titles in the kitchen one night, and he landed on this one. It sounded catchy, or so we thought. I wanted to, needed to pull people in right away, while I was trying to find an agent, and then sell the book. It worked; people responded to it.

What I hadn't really thought about at the time I chose it was how much it resonates. Now I realize that it captures the idea of the dual nature of and danger of the beautiful façade my mother tried so hard to create: something that looks elegant but underneath is quite frightening and unstable. There are also the obvious parallels between our relationships and the complex nature of fire itself—comforting, destructive, explosive, and short-lived. And, of course, the clothes that are pervasive in the story and that meant so much to my mother as a sign of her achievement and a disguise for who she felt she had been. And they were so beautiful, too.

You've appeared on television, in regional theater, and on Broadway. Can you identify one role you've played that has stayed with you over the years?

It would most likely be Frankie in *The Member of the Wedding* by Carson McCullers. She is a lonely, imaginative girl who wants desperately to belong to something. She just aches all over. I always identified with Frankie's search for her identity, and her deep desire to grow. Coincidentally, my stepfather, Oliver Rea, produced the original Broadway production in 1950, with Ethel Waters and Julie Harris as Frankie.

One of your teachers in London, Mr. Jesse, advises, "Life is short, and one musn't squander one's talents, don't you agree?" (page 76). What would you say to Mr. Jesse today if you crossed paths with him?

I would thank him for his encouragement, for teaching me to love words, and for showing me so many beautiful and useful things. And I would tell him that I have tried to live up to his expectations for life.

What can you tell us about the process of writing Chanel Bonfire? Did you look through photo albums or use other methods to refresh your memory?

I did look at photos, of course, the ones that I have. Unfortunately, most of the ones of my teen years were destroyed by my mother. And I listened to music from the time period I was working in. During the first section of the book, 1960s in Manhattan, it was Astrud Gilberto and Frank Sinatra. Then, in early-1970s London, it was T. Rex, David Bowie, and Elton John. Late-seventies Boston was Cheap Trick, Tom Petty, Human Sexual Response, and Madness, of course. Music can really trigger memories for me.

I think I got this method from when I was acting; I'd pick a song or an album that I felt was the sound track to the character I was playing.

What are you working on now? Will there be a follow-up to Chanel Bonfire?

I am working on the sequel to Chanel Bonfire. The girl without a road map for life finds herself in the gritty, dangerous, exciting nadir of downtown New York City. As in *Chanel*, it's darkly funny and terribly misguided—an eighties party girl looking for love in all the wrong places, with a thrift store wardrobe, punk rockers, buzz cuts, drug parties, cross-dressing, birth control issues, and run-ins with the FBI. It's the story of a young actress in New York in the early 1980s, not only searching for Mr. Right, but also for an identity, a job, and maybe a free meal. Oh, and she has a crazy mother.